LEGEND: A CHILDHOOD DREAM

LEGEND:
A CHILDHOOD DREAM

by Lawrence Ryan and
Stephen Webb

Connor Court Publishing

Connor Court Publishing Pty Ltd

Copyright © Lawrence Ryan 2015

ALL RIGHTS RESERVED. This book contains material protected under International and Federal Copyright Laws and Treaties. Any unauthorised reprint or use of this material is prohibited. No part of this book may be reproduced or transmitted in any form or by any means, electronic or mechanical, including photocopying, recording, or by any information storage and retrieval system without express written permission from the publisher.

PO Box 224W
Ballarat VIC 3350
sales@connorcourt.com
www.connorcourt.com

ISBN: 9781925138559 (pbk.)
Cover design by Ian James
Printed in Australia

Contents

Run-up	1
1 A Childhood Dream	5
2 Mum, Can I Borrow the Car?	21
3 Stunt School	34
4 Not Nine to Five	42
5 The Legend Begins	52
6 Crash Heard Around the World	64
7 It's Stunt Business	72
8 Leap of Faith	83
9 All the Fun of the Fair	101
10 The Legend Continues	112
11 A Promise is Kept	121
12 That's Going to Leave a Mark	128
13 Guinness World Records	135
14 You're a Hero	142
15 An Angel Appears	151
16 Made in China	160
17 Rebirth of a Legend	172
18 Always Believe in Your Dreams	178
19 You Won't Believe What I Do Next	189
20 The Future	198

Foreword

Lawrence Ryan is a leaping lunatic. And, I confess, I love it. For the fifteen years I've known him, Lawrence has not just been a stuntman but a true class act.

As Australia's very own Evel Knievel, he's part superhero, part gentlemen, part dreamer, partly psychotic. But, far more importantly, he's always entertaining. Every time. Not only a talent on two wheels but one of our greatest showmen. The kind of wonderful old-school showbiz performer who captivates us all with the 'theatre' of his latest elaborate stunt as much as the stunt itself, costume and all.

Before having a Red Bull sticker on a dirt bike was cool, there was Lawrence. Before bikes were even able to jump fifteen buses, there was Lawrence. Trying it anyway. Doing it through (or while) on fire. The kind of entertainer that had audiences in the palm of his hand, performing stunts that begged you to ask: Will he — or won't he — make it? The best part of all, Lawrence wasn't sure himself most of the time. But he did it anyway. Why, I have no idea. But I'm glad he did — and does.

In the current world of over-thought, over-calculated, flawless but endless cut-and-paste Red Bull riders, Lawrence Legend rides alone. A stuntman whose bone-chilling and spectacular stunt failures — equally as much as his many spectacular successes — have earned him the elite status of stunt icon. Lawrence Legend: a true Australian legend.

Grant Denyer

Run-up

The fire lit up with a huge roar and I came flying out the end. 'Put water on me! Put water on me!'

I felt like I was burning.

'Put it out!'

It was June 1997 at the 'Monte Cristo' homestead in Junee. I was twenty-six, eight years into my career as a professional stunt rider, and attempting to break the record for riding through a Tunnel of Fire — one hundred and twenty feet.

Three weeks earlier I'd made a similar attempt but the tunnel failed to ignite.

This time, to make sure the guys lighting the tunnel couldn't make a mistake, I had gerbs — fireworks that produce jets of sparks — to spray the beginning of the tunnel. Even if my crew was unsuccessful the hessian walls would still catch fire. We poured a lot of fuel on the tunnel, a mixture of diesel and petrol, so we knew it was going to burn.

In the centre I also had a nap bomb — a charge of naphthalene mixed with gunpowder that produces a controlled burn. It looks really good. My theory was that, when I was halfway through, the crew would set it off to make it look like I had exploded in the middle of the tunnel. And then I would ride out the other end.

I set it up and Dad was to do the detonation.

There were two channels for the wiring: one for the sparklers and the other for the big bang. I was ready to go. The crew had doused me with water. Sticks were lit ready to set the tunnel on fire. I gave the nod and took off and Dad pressed the first button. But I had wired it the wrong way. Instead of sparklers there was thunder.

The guys didn't even get to the tunnel to light it. It just went up in a ball of flames. We had a farmer's truck next to the tunnel ready to pour water if I came out the side. The heat was so intense they had to drop the hose and back off.

I knew straight away what had happened: 'Oh God, I've to go. I'm not going to get another chance at this.'

I just went for it.

'This is it, Lawrence. If you second-guess yourself now you're going to be dead.'

It is only a quick trip through a Tunnel of Fire but it seems to last for ages.

I had painted a line down the centre as a guide. That was useless because as soon as I entered the tunnel I could see nothing. There was fire rising from the ground, fire bursting in from the sides. It was a storm of flames. As far as I could tell there was no tunnel.

It was no time for hesitation.

All I could do was ride in a straight line and not back off.

It was blisteringly hot. I was wearing my Levi's jeans with a stripe up the side. My leather jacket. A vest underneath. A thermal vest to keep the radiant heat away. A balaclava, leather gloves and helmet. My undergarments were soaked. Moments earlier I was dripping wet in the middle of winter. Freezing. But not now.

The flames were licking me so closely the bottom of my helmet melted. The leather of my gloves was so taut as my fingers gripped the handlebars that the heat from the fire burnt my knuckles. The fire was so intense it shrunk my leathers, crystallised the visor and started to melt the wires on the bike.

When I first emerged from the extreme heat to the winter cold I thought I must have still been in the tunnel. My shrinking leathers had brought the heat and steam closer to my body. It was more painful on the other side than it was in the fire.

I only knew I was out of the tunnel because instead of bright orange and a spectrum of reds I could see blue sky. I slid the bike and dropped it because I didn't know if the bike was on fire or what had happened. People raced over with a fire extinguisher. I screamed out, thinking I was still ablaze.

But they were standing over me and could see I wasn't. Others came over with buckets of water and started pouring it down my sleeves. My jacket had shrunk two sizes smaller and was stuck on me.

Dad was shaking. He said he had never been as scared as when the bomb went off. He hadn't expected that kind of fire. He thought he did something wrong when he pressed the button and it blew.

All I was worried about was if I had the record.

With people huddled round me and the heat abated, the first thing I said was, 'Well, did I get it?'

Dad's friend reached down, 'Of course you did.'

1
A Childhood Dream

Is a stunt rider born or made? Was there always an inner stunt man lurking in my genes?

I was three when I told my dad I wanted to be a stuntman.

Teacher, police officer, truck driver — these seemed okay occupations for other kids to aspire to but I knew they were tame compared to my dream.

By ten I was into serious, self-guided practice to reach my goal — and, if my parents had let me, that would have involved riding through fire.

It all started in a little town in rural Australia called Junee ...

On March 28, 1971, I was one of the last children to be born in Junee District Hospital, before they stopped delivering children at Junee and sent expectant mothers to Wagga Wagga Base Hospital, forty-five kilometres away.

I love to tell people my coming into the world was the reason. I am the only boy in our family, the youngest of five children with four older sisters. Between the youngest sister and me there is a seven-year gap — an accident or the consequence of Mum and Dad getting a new mattress.

Junee is located in the Riverina, an agricultural region in the south-west of New South Wales. It rarely gets so cold in Junee that it snows, though it has snowed twice. It is cold, green and lush in winter and summers are hot, dry and dusty.

In 1971 the sign on the outskirts of town said Junee's population was three thousand people. The figure flatlined for thirty years — typical of long-term population erosion in the Australian wheat belt and the decline of the rail-based economy — but the sign now says four thousand and the population of the wider district is over six thousand. The town is known for its crops, lamb, railway repair facilities and tourist attractions, including the 'Monte Cristo' homestead, where I was raised. The house operates as a museum, antique store … and Australia's most haunted home.

Dad, Reg Ryan, was a tailor by trade when he bought 'Monte Cristo' in 1963. The homestead, a double-story late-Victorian manor, was constructed in 1885 by local pioneer Christopher William Crawley on a hill overlooking the town. Crawley acquired land in the area in 1876 and struggled as a farmer until his fortunes changed when the Great Southern Railway Line opened in 1878. He obtained a license and built the Railway Hotel opposite the soon to be bustling railway station and along with the rest of the township began to benefit from the influx of travellers and agricultural trade. Crawley's wealth and land holdings increased dramatically. A devout Roman Catholic, he donated a parcel of land to the church and helped finance important civic projects. 'Monte Cristo' (Mount of Christ) was an ever-present symbol of his wealth and social status.

Crawley died in 1910 but the Crawley family lived at 'Monte Cristo' until 1948. Caretakers remained to stop squatters coming into the empty house. Unfortunately the last caretaker was shot by a local boy who had watched the movie *Psycho* three times. After the third time he acquired a shotgun, went up to the caretaker's cottage and knocked at the door. When the caretaker answered, the boy shot him. No-one wanted the job after that. It took eighteen months for the once-magnificent house to be vandalised and reduced to a brick shell.

The caretaker's death followed several others at 'Monte Cristo', each contributing to the homestead's ghostly reputation. Other tragic incidents included the long imprisonment of a mentally impaired man, a young child fatally falling down the stairs, a maid toppling from the balcony and a stable boy burning to death. Mrs Crawley is said to have never left the house.

Dad once dreamed that he lived in a double-storey house on a hill with an outcrop of rock out the front. He spotted 'Monte Cristo' while waiting in Junee after taking a girl there to teach dancing. When he saw 'Monte Cristo', he recognised it from his dream. He had to own it.

It took him eight years to negotiate buying it because it was left to the estate and half the family wanted to sell and the other half did not. He took some photos of the dilapidated state of the homestead and showed them to the reluctant family members. That convinced them to sell.

Dad purchased 'Monte Cristo' as a house for the family, not to be used as a museum. He had no idea there were hauntings. He moved in with no electricity, no running water, not a pane of glass in any door or window. Mum and Dad had three daughters then and my Mum, Olive, was five months pregnant with the fourth. For some reason she didn't want to move in.

But Dad was a visionary. He could see potential in the place: 'Can't you picture this? A coat of paint here, a picture there? It will be fantastic!'

Mum deserves a medal.

Their first load of furniture came from St Vincent de Paul in Wagga Wagga; they had moved in with two blow-up beds, single beds for two girls, a cot for the baby and two chairs. Dad was working for a welder, learning how to weld so he could reconstruct all the cast iron from the balconies. Dad was going to ask his boss for help to take the furniture home but the guy from Vinnies said he was there to help.

When he saw the house he said, 'But you've got no glass in the windows.'

Dad said he was working on it.

The guy from Vinnies said they were the most deserving case he'd ever seen.

It was eighteen months before they could afford to get French doors for the entrance onto the top balcony. The wind would howl down the staircase and bats flew in. Mum had long hair and dreaded bats getting tangled in it. Dad had put canvas up to cover the windows but one had a burn hole in it. One night Mum, five months pregnant and lying on a single blow-up bed, had just fallen asleep when three bats flew in through the hole. Dad knew if he had woken Mum she would have run out and never come back.

Larger than life

Dad's father was a railway worker, so Dad had moved around a fair bit, even sleeping in a tent on dirt floors beside the railway tracks.

He learned his trade in the army, which he joined before he realised it was hard work and people yelled at you all the time. So he served his country sartorially — he became a tailor. Pretty soon, by necessity, he was a jack of all trades. He was a bricklayer, a wheelwright — he could make a carriage wheel from scratch — he could do electrical work. You name it, he would do it because he couldn't afford to pay anyone else to do it. That was his attitude all through life: 'Why pay someone to do something if you can do it yourself. Do it properly yourself the first time.'

When Mum's parents were divorced she lived briefly with a stepmother who was only ten years older than her. They didn't get on so she moved in with an aunt in Sydney who had eleven other children. Mum says she went for the weekend and stayed five years. From there she moved to Wagga Wagga. Having worked as a seamstress in Sydney, she was offered a job with Dad. She was then twenty-three and he was nineteen. She was older than her boss. Dad wasn't able to pay proper wages so she got a job at the confectionary counter at Woolworths. Dad, though, wanted to marry her and asked her to wait two years. She waited and they married.

Mum now tells people she went from working for Dad for a pittance to sleeping with him and getting paid nothing.

Although he was a tailor, Dad became an antique dealer for the sole purpose of refurbishing the house. Back then few people collected antique furniture; they were more likely to inherit their grandparents' house furniture and throw it out because they couldn't give it away. The running joke at our house was that Dad would go to the tip with one load of rubbish and come back with two.

Then, in the 1980s, furniture from the 1880s and earlier became popular. There was a trend for people with a bit of money — lawyers, doctors — to invest in artwork and antique furniture. Dad quickly realised this and got a licence to wheel and deal in second-hand furniture. He would make three trips a year to London, bringing back a container-load of furniture, which he'd sell to professionals and wealthy farmers from the ballroom at the back of 'Monte Cristo'. On many trips within Australia, even holidays, we'd go away in a station wagon and come home with me lying on one side next to a big wardrobe.

Our family did it tough until the antique business started to thrive and 'Monte Cristo' attracted more tourists, weddings and parties, for which we catered in the homestead's function hall. From the early eighties it was always busy but during my childhood from 1971, while I was oblivious to our financial problems, my sisters knew times were hard. They had to climb on the roof to help paint the chimneys and carry furniture upstairs. Dad would say they shouldn't complain because they went on to win first place in shot put at the school carnivals.

I remember Dad being larger than life. He was always busy; there was always something happening. I could go to school in the morning and come home in the afternoon and there'd be a wall missing or one put up. It was exciting, wondering what else would have changed. There might be a hole or trench dug for some wiring; and that was fun because then I could play in it.

Dad loved horse-drawn vehicles so much we once had eighty carriages on the property. He taught himself to be a wheelwright because he couldn't afford to pay someone to restore the carriages. He met some of the old-timers who originally made carriage wheels for a living, bought out a couple of blacksmith shops with tools and equipment and taught himself to make carriage wheels. As a teenager I helped him — we made hundreds of wheels.

In the early days we would hire the carriages for weddings. From the ages of ten to fourteen I was a footman, hopping off the back of the carriages to open the doors for the bridal parties. When insurance costs rose and we had no more horses on the property hiring carriages became impractical. In 1999 we sold forty at auction. The remainder are on display in the museum.

Dad was a kind person but strict. If you pushed his buttons you'd know about it. He was large framed with wide shoulders like me. I wasn't afraid of him, just respectful and aware of likely consequences for crossing the boundaries. I wasn't allowed to swear; there was never any swearing. I might have a got a belting once or twice but if you asked my sisters they'd say I never got the hiding I deserved.

When he was a boy Dad imagined owning a Rolls Royce — it would have his initials on it RR: Reg Ryan. By the time I was a teenager, he had seven houses and flats in Junee, plus a bank building with an old safe. He wheeled and dealed some carriages for an old 1923 model

Rolls and liked to tell people he'd been driving past his bank in his Rolls Royce.

Dad also owned the Junee Hotel (formerly Crawley's Railway Hotel) for a couple of years. He grew the business from two kegs a week to seventeen kegs a week.

In my blood

I'm like my Dad in many ways. We were built the same way. I find it hard to sit on a beach and just look out at the ocean; I love to do it but I get bored after ten minutes. I'd rather be doing something.

The main difference between us was that Dad's passion was for 'Monte Cristo' and mine was for stunt work. Dad remembered me coming to him when I was three and saying I wanted to be stuntman. 'That's great,' he said, wondering why I didn't want to be a fireman or policeman like other kids.

Dad wasn't interested in stunt driving. He missed out on the 'stunt gene'. It was actually his brother, who I was named after — Neville Lawrence Ryan — who was a car nut. He had all the books and loved to tinker with things. Dad said if he hadn't died before I was born I would have been spoilt rotten. He would have taken me under his wing. My first motorbike would have been standing by my crib. As it turned out I didn't get my first motorbike until I was fourteen.

What I did have was pushbikes. I grew up watching *That's Incredible*, an American television show in the early eighties hosted by John Davidson, Fran Tarkenton and Cathy Lee Crosby. Each week they would feature a stunt person, often doing something extremely dangerous. By the time they started adding the caption 'Do Not Try This Yourself' it was too late. I spent most of my spare time in the back yard trying to do something I saw on television. I just thought, 'I can do that.' My limited equipment didn't hold me back: I improvised stunts for pushbikes and billycarts, with old paint cans and planks lined up for ramps. It was very much trial and error.

Three generations before me have been involved in motorbikes and my nephew has been to shows and ridden with me but we had no idea of the stunt connection to the family until I started my stunt career in 1989. Out of the blue, Mum said, 'My uncles used to ride in the army display riding team.'

'Really?'

'Oh, yes, three of them did.'

Then Dad thought back and said, 'You know your grandfather, he used to be a fill-in rider for the Globe of Death and the Wall of Death. And did you know your great-grandparents used to race motorcycles?'

How rare it must have been back then for a woman to race a motorcycle!

Although Dad wasn't into stunts he did have one bike adventure — on a penny-farthing. Dad once got a gunsmith in town to re-spoke the bike's wheels. When it was finished, instead of loading it into a trailer and bringing it home, Dad decided to ride it home. The driveway to 'Monte Cristo' was long and steep, down into a valley and up towards the house. On the downhill run there was a sharp corner. Dad rode the penny-farthing down the hill, but the new leather on the seat was soft and stretchy; he used the pedals to slow the bike but, straining backwards, slipped on the leather, fell off and broke his arm.

After that he stopped riding the penny-farthing and I took over. I enjoyed riding it, even as a teenager.

We have a book about penny-farthings with a whole chapter on 'how to impress the ladies'. One of the recommended moves is to throw your leg over the handlebars and dismount to the side. When I tried the manoeuvre my weight went too far forward and I ended

My father, Reginald Ryan, riding a penny farthing bike at our home 'Monte Cristo' in the early '70s.

My mother, Olive (Summerell) Ryan, sitting on a visiting friend's motorcycle before she met my father. Notice the letters on the number plate. A little bit spooky!

In the bloodline. My great uncle, Albert Wedge, riding this BSA as part of the army display team in Palestine.

Father Reg and my very first ride.

up spinning on the axis of the front wheel and falling on my face in front of the bike — surely not a way to win the admiration of the 'ladies'. And there were more challenges than suavely mounting and dismounting. Our backyard was strewn with bindi-eyes, a weed with burs like thumbtacks. The bike's big wheel collected the burs while I was going straight and de-burred itself on the inside of my leg when I turned a corner.

I'm still fond of an old photograph of Dad standing beside that bike with me, a toddler, perched on top.

As a child, my television diet was comprised of *Knight Rider*, *The Fall Guy* and *The A-Team* — all the highly action packed shows. That's where my passion lay.

Growing up with four sisters a lot older than me, I had to occupy myself, which wasn't hard on a big property with lots of buildings and carriages. I could play cowboys and Indians because we had horse-drawn vehicles on the property, or imagine the house was an enormous spaceship. I would run around play-acting, often by myself. Sometimes cousins from Sydney would visit but rarely did friends from town come to play. It wasn't until I was thirteen or fourteen that friends came up for BMX riding and jumping. And it wasn't until I got my first motorbike and decided to build some ramps and jump it that a couple of mates came up to watch. Since I landed it and didn't kill myself, the next day I was the talk of the school. After that, any time I did anything on a weekend I'd have twenty-odd friends up to see what we could wreck. We got up to a bit of mischief but nothing most kids didn't do at the time.

Back then there was no internet, no mobile phones; we didn't worry about children getting abducted. I was very much an outdoor kid, always on the go. Digging holes to make tunnels. Climbing into tree houses. That was the staple. I went out when it got light and got back before it got dark. I rarely saw my parents. I'd come home to get something to eat and then fly out again. I wore myself out silly and went to bed. If I had to play inside, it was usually Lego, using my imagination to build things.

Nobody really worried. That's how my childhood was: unsupervised mayhem. I'd be out the back paddock with pushbikes or motorbikes. The only time I ever worried Mum and Dad was when I was about ten and built a ramp for my pushbike and erected some metal fence posts, star pickets, attached some sticks and hung big sheets of newspaper across them. My parents had been watching so when I went up to the house to ask for matches they asked, 'What are they for?'

'I'm going to light that on fire and ride through it.'

'Don't you think that's a bit silly? What happens if you catch fire?'

At the bottom of that hill we have a little pond. I said, 'Well if I catch on fire I'll keep riding into the pond and put myself out.'

I didn't get the matches.

I have a photo of that jump because a bus group of tourists came to see 'Monte Cristo' and the bus driver photographed me jumping through a wall of paper.

Nothing changed as I grew older. Mum would come out and yell, 'Why can I smell fire? What are you burning down the back?' Or, 'What's that big bang that just went off?' I was just trying to work out how to make pyrotechnics go off as spectacularly as they did in the movies.

'It's just a car backfiring.'

My kids always laugh when they see the warnings: 'Don't try this at home'.

'See that Dad? It says you are not allowed to try that at home.'

I say, 'That doesn't apply to me.'

A golden childhood

I spent a lot of time alone as a young child but didn't need an imaginary friend. Being in a house with a reputation for having so many spirits I always sensed there was someone around me, someone was with me.

When I was ten I had a dog called Bandit. He was a blue healer/kelpie cross with a black mask on his face. People thought that's how he got his name but I really named him after *Smokey and the Bandit*, starring Burt Reynolds, who led police on a merry chase across the country in a black Pontiac. The director of that film, Hal Needham, a legendary stuntman, used four modified black Pontiac Firebird Trans Ams for the stunt work.

Bandit became a close companion when my sisters were no longer around. I kept him for ten years. My sisters used to have pet birds and my mother also had a dog until she backed over him in the car taking us to school one morning. But my parents came from an era where they struggled for food and didn't believe in spending money on pets. They were fed scraps and had to fend for themselves.

I rode horses when I was a boy and can still ride now but would rather not have anything to do with the animals. My sisters tell me that when I was small I used to have a mop bucket to stand on to climb onto a horse. It was a placid animal and I don't remember ever being hurt but I still don't like horses. You fall off them, they tread on your head, they stomp up and down on you and then they walk off. I'd much rather ride something that didn't make plans for itself.

My parents remained in Junee. If you sent them away for a week they were back in two days because they couldn't stay away from the house. Well, Dad couldn't. They lived in a private section of 'Monte Cristo', with an en suite and a modern TV room, away from the general public and the tourists coming through. The dining room and bedrooms are still used if we have relatives or friends staying.

I like living in Junee. It is a very pretty, quiet town. I wouldn't live anywhere else; which is why I bought land from Mum and Dad. The Crawley land that Mum and Dad bought, where we used to run horses and grow some grain, three hundred metres from 'Monte Cristo', is where I have built my home. The land also has dirt ramps and timber and metal ramps and a tar oval track, where I practise two-wheel driving. It's the one-stop shop for my rehearsal and photo shoots.

'Monte Cristo' is still our house but more a museum than our home. My partner Sophia and I look after our guests, as Mum and Dad had done for most of the twenty-first century. In addition to tours of the house during the week, we do a bed and breakfast on Saturday nights for up to twenty guests. We tell ghost stories and take them through the house by candlelight. And then they stay the night — in the house. I lead the tours and Sophia does the cooking. And any friends or family who stand still long enough get to strip beds, make beds and help prepare for the next weekend.

Mum and Dad always made friends and visitors feel welcome. People walking in the door were always greeted with a smile. Mum and Dad would help anyone out.

When people come to the front door of 'Monte Cristo' the kids are scared and ask if they will see any ghosts. We say, 'No, you'll be right. But, when you get to the front door and press the doorbell, a creepy old lady might answer it. That's just my Mum.' That puts a smile on their faces but I have to say, 'Don't you tell my Mum I said that, though.'

All four of my sisters were entered in Miss Showgirl in Junee. Two of them won. Mum says they wouldn't take me … even though she kept my blond hair long when I was little and people kept mistaking me for a girl.

Mum has a very dry sense of humour. It comes across as mean and scary but she's really the opposite of that. My sisters' friends joke about how scared they were of my Mum; they didn't worry about my Dad. Mum comes from an era when all old people seemed to be grumpy. They all had that mannerism; they were bred that way. They did things a lot tougher, of course. She has a heart of gold but can't hug you; she grew up not getting hugs. My parents didn't do that sort of thing. My sisters and I now crave attention and for someone to hug us because I don't think we got it as kids. It was not until they were older with grandchildren that there were more hugs in the family.

I'm not as close to my sisters as I was when I was very little. As they got older I became something of a plaything for them. At other times it seemed as though I had four extra mothers. Things only improved financially for the family after I came along and the hard work on the house was completed. So I became the spoilt one, the golden child, the one who was looked after better. My sisters think I'm just a kid, still showing off, and have never taken my stunt work seriously.

Dad once showed me how to weld and then I had to teach myself. I cut cars up and put roll bars on them, with no idea what I was doing. I tried whatever I could do to make a stunt car that I could tip over. I look back and think, 'How didn't I kill myself?' But there was no-one to guide me or show me. No-one saying, 'Well, how about we help you, Lawrence, because that's a little bit dangerous' or 'Have you thought about this?'

I read about a survey in America where people of my generation said they believed they were the last of a golden childhood, where kids were free to be kids. The trends must be similar in Australia: in the last forty years we've lost our sense of community. Mothers can work, neighbours talk less over the back fence, there's more divorce, more absent fathers. The media generate fear. Parents think their children are fragile, too tender to play outside on their own or to tackle risky activities.

From my experience, I'd tend to agree with the American columnist who thought a happy medium would be the ideal. There would be closer ties between parents and children and the recognition that part of being a good, caring parent is letting children discover things on their own.

Dad died in July 2014, while I was working on this book. He said he wanted to be the next ghost at 'Monte Cristo'. He was going to have fun.

2
MUM, CAN I BORROW THE CAR?

I often say in media interviews that my stunts are dangerous and people shouldn't try them at home. It's not advice I would have followed as a child. I tried everything.

My very first stunt (unless you count taking off down the hill, wading chest deep through a swamp and somehow ending up on a neighbour's doorstep) involved my first pushbike, a Christmas present when I was four years old. Back then when we got a Christmas present it was just a *single* present. Not like today when some kids get dozens of gifts.

That year I had to follow a string tied to the Christmas tree, through the hallways of 'Monte Cristo', out onto the verandah and around to a side room, where I found a little red pushbike with trainer wheels. I thought the bike was pretty special. I rode it everywhere.

By the following March I was five and getting proficient at riding. I bent the training wheels up because I was hardly using them. Dad wanted to take the training wheels off completely. I thought, 'That's not good; that means I can fall over.' I kicked up a stink but Dad insisted. I was devastated. 'Now you've ruined everything!'

I had a cunning plan. I pushed the bike around to a grassed area at the side of the house, lay down on the ground, pulled the bike on top of me and started to cry, intending that my parents would look out and see me, think I'd hurt myself badly and put the training wheels back on. But Mum and Dad had been sitting in the sunroom at the back of the house, having a cup of tea, and had seen everything. They came out and said, 'No. Stop crying. Stop being silly. We saw you. You'll live.'

So it was my parents' fault that I embarked on my daredevil career — I had to be brave and adventurous whether I wanted to or not.

That was also my first lesson in planning for contingencies when preparing stunts.

Despite my reservations about losing my training wheels, I never had any serious pushbike accidents; just the many occasions I'd lose skin off the palms of my hands and my nose after washing out cornering on the loose clay surface. Those bumps and bruises were typical for kids back then, falling off things or out of trees. Today Community Services would be around wondering if your parents had been beating you.

Back then the bikes I jumped ramps on were dragsters, with banana handlebars and a bar up the back of the seat. It wasn't until the early eighties that I had my first BMX bike, the off-road bike used for racing and stunt riding. In 1982 the BMX craze was in full swing. In Junee they built a BMX track with dirt piles for the local kids and organised races with ribbons for the winners. I remember competing twice there. A mate from school had a flasher, lighter bike and always beat me. He would do double jumps that I was scared to do. I still have a ribbon for coming second.

The first ramp I built for a dragster jump was a metal barbecue plate with a slight bow. I worked out that, if I put it upside down with a couple of bricks under it, when I rode onto the plate it would flex, pop in and then pop out, helping to throw the bike off the jump. I carried that ramp everywhere.

I used to gauge height and how good you were by the number of house bricks you stacked under the ramp ... until it got too steep and the bricks would fall over. Then I got the top of a shipping crate and half a dozen planks about a metre and a half long, joined by two pieces of wood, which meant I could stack more bricks beneath the ramp.

I built a BMX track in our front yard, with the ramp raised an impressive six-bricks high. But one morning I flipped and landed on my tail bone, winding myself. It felt like I had broken my back. It was horrifying. I thought I was paralysed and screamed out. But when my sister leaned over the balcony wondering what all the noise was about, I acted brave, 'No, no, I'm all right.'

I lost a lot of skin on BMX bikes.

When I first built a ramp to jump over our pond I got my mate Darren to do it. I was too scared. (I have since given him a photo from that day — no helmet, landing short with water spraying up everywhere — signed to 'A stuntman's stuntman' because he was brave enough to do it before I tried.)

I set up that jump again at a birthday party and another mate tried it on my bike, flipped over backwards and hurt his back. I got in trouble for that.

I have an aerial photograph of the property back then and you can see all my ramps stacked up in a corner of the car park area. One ramp I was proud of was a timber ramp from my primary school, made to slide across stairs for a girl in a wheelchair. When she left, a friend got hold of it and gave it to me. It was only particle board and, after several years left out in the rain, it fell apart but we have great photos of the jumps we did with it. Some were criss-cross jumps, one after the other or one sliding under another. I was pretty imaginative and still managed to rope my mates into those things. We didn't wear helmets and my mates wore only shorts and T-shirts — but I didn't want to take more skin off so always wore long pants and jackets.

We also attempted stunts in billycarts. We watched the annual Bathurst 1000 touring car race, with drivers like Peter Brock and Dick Johnson, and thought race cars looked fun. Billycarts were the closest we could get. One that I made had a fruit crate as a nose.

The big dirt hill in front of 'Monte Cristo' was perfect for racing billycarts. We organised a competition with prizes but my billycart was the slowest. Instead of racing, I got my mates to push me down the hill and used the barbecue plate to launch the billycart. It didn't work too well. I left the seat when the cart left the ground, then it landed and I landed on it. We had one with a metal frame, a string to steer, and lawnmower wheels on front and back. There was no seat so we used a cast metal tractor implement seat, which Dad bolted on for me. That's what I hit when I returned to earth after flying off the ramp.

There were many days spent dragging billycarts up and down hills. Lord knows why I wasn't a lot fitter.

I was a chubby kid, not very athletic, but I played basketball, soccer, cricket and football when I got older. I never stuck with any one sport because they bored me. Team sports didn't suit me because I wanted to be in the action. In soccer you had to pass the ball and couldn't keep running with it yourself. In cricket you had to stand out in a paddock for half a day doing nothing — though I enjoyed the theatre of running and diving for the catch: much more stunt-like!

I played football for the Junee Diesels, a year below Laurie Daley, the Australian rugby league representative player and New South Wales State of Origin coach. It seemed that football was mostly about fights and who could beat up whom. Because my birthday was in March I was about six months younger than most of my friends at school. I could play in my own age bracket but all my friends played in the year above. I was big enough to play second row with them but didn't enjoy getting pummelled and knocked around. Jumping motor bikes seemed safer.

Painful memories

My ideas for ramps came from *That's Incredible* and similar TV shows. One stunt guy on *That's Incredible* had a bike he tried to jump over a row of cars. He came down the ramp, was pulled off the bike and the bike exploded. It looked great but it was a special effect, using a deceleration cable to yank him off the bike so he'd fall safely onto boxes behind the cars, while explosives were set off on the bike. It looked awesome and I was inspired. Monkey see, monkey do.

The closest I had to a deceleration cable was half a dozen octopus straps and my father's belt tied around my waist, with a piece of string tied around a tree. My theory was if I rode away quickly enough it would have the desired effect and I could work up to doing a jump. On the first attempt I rode off at full pelt and, when the belt took up the slack, I was yanked off the bike. The belt was only an inch and a half thick; it didn't do my stomach any good but I thought it wasn't too bad. The next time I tried to ride a bit faster but the string broke and the octopus straps flicked up and whipped me in the spine.

I should have learned from an earlier stunt involving a rope around my waist. I had climbed a peppercorn tree playing mountaineers, with the rope around my waist like a belaying rope that climbers used to prevent themselves falling off cliffs. Very 'scientifically' I had worked out that, if I measured the rope tied to a branch and reaching down to the ground, I could jump out of the tree and it wouldn't hang me up. I hadn't factored in the drastic shortening of the rope when I tied it around me. I jumped out of the tree and the rope nearly cut me in half; I could just get a toe to the ground to relieve some of the pressure.

I was also inspired by a stunt where a guy was pushed down a hill in two large tractor tubes tied together, onto a ramp and over a limousine. It was a quirky stunt, using a car each side of the tubes to guide them onto the ramp. I thought, 'That's doable. I can find some tubes.'

I couldn't find tubes but we did have a corrugated iron water tank. My mates came over one weekend and we put mattresses in the tank. I climbed through the little hole at one end and had them roll me down the hill. I discovered then that I get motion sickness something chronic. If I can't see the horizon I get violently ill. When they rolled me down the hill it seemed like it would never stop. It wasn't very fast but I had no further thought about trying it over a ramp, especially after I cut myself on the jagged edge of a hole punched in the side of the tank. I still have the scar on my hand from the gash inflicted as I tried to stop myself flopping around. And I can still see the blood going around with me.

There may have been cuts and plenty of bruises but I never broke anything. I had mates with broken arms and legs but the worst thing I managed as a kid was in year six in 1982 … and it didn't involve a stunt. I was playing cowboys and Indians with a mate in an old combine harvester. One outlet on the machine was surrounded by spikes to hold the hessian bags as they were filled with grain. I was underneath it shooting at my mate and stood up too quick, catching my head on the spikes. I had four stitches to show off at school.

Smoke on the water

There was never a dull moment at our place. It was always an adventure. We lived on a property with open space and no-one behind us. It's all subdivision now but then you could shoot a .22 rifle up the back yard and not hit anything. My friends lived in town with neighbours over the back fence. My place was the place to hang out. We had a lot more freedom and not much supervision.

Mum and Dad were always busy; there was always something going on. There was no time to mind us. I entertained myself and they didn't have to worry as long as I came home at night. My friends' parents used to complain to Mum and Dad about how dirty they would be when they came home from my place, dragging things around and digging holes and making jumps.

There was always an adventure. There was never a moment we weren't out doing something … something that we probably shouldn't be doing.

Like many kids I thought stories about the bushranger Ned Kelly and his armour were exciting. When I was twelve I worked out how to make Ned Kelly helmets that we could shoot with air rifles without getting badly hurt. We used BMX goggles to protect our eyes when we shot one another with paper spit balls. Thinking back on it now, it was not a smart idea.

A Christmas present from Mum and Dad. My first bike and what started it all.

Wall of fire! No matches so a wall of paper. (Photo taken by visiting bus driver).

Aged 15 and geared up for my second ever motorcycle jump over a car. A newer bike with more suspension.

Overshooting the landing by a mile.

I didn't wise up as a teenager. I kept the slug gun in my bedroom, which, since it was an old house, I sometimes shared with mice. If I saw one I would get the gun and kill it. I even had a target set up in my room. Once I turned my radio off by shooting the metal toggle switch on top — though breaking the switch off. Another day I tested my marksmanship by trying to hit the head of a nail that was holding up a shelf in my wardrobe. I had one eye closed and the other looking through the scope. It might have been a fluke but I hit the nail and the slug ricocheted back and hit me on the closed eye. I realised how lucky I was. You don't always think things through too rationally when you are a teenager. But I learned not to shoot my gun inside after that.

Outside activities also invited mishaps: wooden sword fights with shields I decorated, dirt clod fights and games of dare, like shooting arrows into the air to see who would wait and who would run away before the arrows came down.

I met a kid once whose parents bought a motel in town. His brother dug deep holes in the backyard and covered them with planks. It was like an underground cubby house. It seemed like another good idea so I went home and started digging holes in the bushes behind our house. Pretty soon I had a network of trenches covered in planks that we could crawl through by candle light. It was fun for us but could have ended in tragedy if someone had driven a car over us.

We have a pool at 'Monte Cristo' that Dad dug out by hand and built himself — one of the first concrete, in-ground pools. It was good for swimming in the summer but also ideal for building ramps and jumping into on pushbikes. When I got older I set myself on fire before jumping in.

Other water sports included jumping a BMX bike over the pond in the front paddock, putting some mates in a boat and jumping them and then using some petrol to set the water on fire and jumping that.

I was fifteen when fireworks were banned for sale to the public. We only had access to the safer version of the big crackers my relatives used to blow up mail boxes. We could still tie them together or pull them apart and repackage them to make something destructive. And every farmer had detonating cord and the explosives used for blowing up tree stumps. While I didn't have access to that I knew plenty of people who did. As a kid I could go into K-Mart and buy shotgun shells for rabbit shooting. Often I would come home and cut them in half and get the gunpowder to make things that went 'Bang!'

Half a dozen of us would gather in the back paddock with old car bonnets up as shields, lighting fireworks and high-tailing it out of the way. We used dodgy fuses from fireworks that would only burn down so far until someone had to go in to check them, trudging closer with a bonnet raised for protection. I have a photograph of two friends who had realised the fuse was still smouldering and turned in full sprint away from the explosion with the bonnet still standing. The next shot is of a Milo can launching skywards.

It's a marvel some of those kids growing up in the seventies and eighties are still alive. If my son is reading this he'll be wondering why he gets in trouble for doing merely silly things when I used to do such completely stupid things.

Nowadays we have to worry about what our kids are doing on social media. I don't let my son wander around town like we used to do. If we went to town we would hang around a mate's place or take our bikes ten kilometres out of town looking for adventure or to go out yabbying in a dam. No-one would know where we were.

I saw a picture on Facebook of pushbikes parked outside a house. It said, 'Before cell phones, before the internet, this is how we knew where your friends were.' That was so true.

When I first imagined myself as a stunt performer I was interested in bikes and motorbikes but as I got older I realised motorbikes could be dangerous. Mum and Dad said they weren't going to buy me one:

'You hear stories about kids breaking their necks.' I thought they could be right. A car stunt man, that's what I'd be. Cars had roll bars wrapped around them and I'd be strapped in. That would be perfect.

That idea didn't last. When I was thirteen my sister and brother-in-law owned a farm just out of town. I visited them often and he got sick of me driving a ute through the crops and crushing down the wheat.

'I've had enough of that, you've got to learn to ride the motorbike.'

I had ridden a motorbike three years before but it had scared the hell out of me. They had put me on a small bike, a 70, but I didn't understand the concept of changing gears. I just rode around in circles in whatever gear it took off in. I was hanging on so tight my hands had indentations from the grips. I didn't understand it and was afraid I would be stranded out in the middle of a paddock. It was very much trial by fire.

The next time, when I was older, my brother-in-law put me on a beaten up old farm bike, a 125, and my lesson was just starting it up and holding it. He said, 'Right, I'm about to put it in gear.' He jammed his foot on the gear lever, it popped into gear and off I went. 'See ya,' he said.

I spent the day riding around the paddocks and learning how to change gears. And the bug bit me. I was soon out on the bike burning fire breaks with a drip torch, circling myself in with fire. I thought, 'Hello, there's a pile of dirt. I'll just jump the motorbike through that and out the other side.' I did it and thought, 'How cool's this!' That's when I really got the love for motorbikes. I never looked back.

I'll always appreciate the many hours of my childhood spent on farms: learning to drive motorbikes and cars, towing chaser bins during harvest, collecting grain, picking up hay bales and roustabouting.

My first motorbike and the first real stunt

I didn't lose my love for cars but motorbikes were easier and more accessible. Even a second-hand wreck back then was five hundred dollars, whereas I could buy a motorbike for one hundred dollars.

The first bike I had when I was fourteen belonged to my Dad's dad, who passed away. He had bikes and cars, some from the uncle I never met. Dad brought the bikes back to a block of flats he was renting to a mechanic. He left them there for him to fix up. I said to Dad, 'Can I get one of those bikes to see if I can get it going?' I brought it home, cleaned out the carburettor and got it working. It was a 1965 Suzuki 100 road bike. No suspension front or back. Never meant to be jumped. Never meant to be anything. I soon pulled off all the lights and everything I didn't need; even the exhaust pipes so it would sound cooler. I found some old knobby tyres to provide a bit of grip and some handlebars that made it look like a motocross bike.

And that was the bike I decided I was going to jump over Mum's car.

I had no real carpentry skills, just a hammer and nails, and I couldn't afford to buy timber so made a makeshift ramp from the scrap timber that was lying around our house, left over from the constant renovations. Picking through the shed I found some old wardrobe doors: light timber frames with a plywood cover; honeycomb thin and not structurally sound. But I thought, 'This will be good.'

I placed two doors lengthways with a couple of planks. It was narrow but I thought I'd be able to line it up. Then I needed something to support the ramp: my Mum's car, a Toyota Corolla she'd won in a raffle. I dragged the ramp up across the nose of the car with the top resting on the roof. I found some metal trestles to support the planks at the higher end nearer the car but I needed something to reinforce the lower end. I found a couple of house bricks and some paint tins and put them on top of each other. At the other end of the car was an old timber bench and a big piece of plywood — something to take some of the bite out of the landing.

I had a couple of mates with me that weekend. They didn't think it would work but I said, 'Nah, it'll be right.'

I made the run up okay, the ramp held together and I jumped. When I landed, the bike cracked the bench in half, which helped cushion the landing. The muffler bent up around my ear, the frame twisted and the front wheel buckled. But I didn't fall off. My mates were gobsmacked that I was dumb enough to do it: 'Oh man, thought you were dead for sure.'

I just thought, 'That was awesome! How cool's that?'

We joked about it for a while and after everyone disbanded I snuck the bench back, thinking, 'Dad won't notice.' I packed up everything else and put Mum's car away. She didn't know until years later that I used her car to prop the ramp for the first jump.

Really, the jump was just riding over the top and falling down. It's embarrassing to think back on it but none of my friends would have even thought of trying it. Evel Knievel's first known jump was using a Honda 250cc motorcycle to jump a crate of rattlesnakes and two mountain lions.

On Monday at school everyone was talking about it. 'Lawrence did this cool jump …' It was really exciting. But I realised if I was going to continue with better jumps that old bike wasn't going to cut it. So I hunted around for a bike I could jump properly.

I've had many bikes since then, some of them pretty bad. I didn't get my first brand new bike until I was twenty-nine. It was a Honda CR250, a racing dirt bike. I had a second hand CR500 and other 250s before that. Honda for some reason was the bike of choice. I had Suzukis before, but kept with Honda as a theme because I had a theory that, if you didn't chop and change bikes and uniforms, people would remember who you were. So I had a stable of Honda bikes for many years.

3

STUNT SCHOOL

School was hard because I am dyslexic. I didn't notice I was different with my dyslexia until year six when teachers said I was behind in my reading and writing skills. I was taken to a university to see a therapist to work out why I was having trouble. They made me read tongue-twister books. When the results came back I had a reading level two years younger than me but a comprehension level two years older. My thinking was all right; I just couldn't read or put it down on paper.

It wasn't until I was in high school that they identified the cause. I can see words clearly, I know what I am reading, but it gets jumbled in my head. Then I didn't see it as a big problem; I just had trouble reading and writing and spelling. Of course, they are things school thinks are important.

In high school I struggled. My writing was almost like shorthand. I knew what I was writing and could read it back but if someone else looked at it they'd say I couldn't spell to save my life. I was an average student — really good at maths — but my mind was always on adventure; what I was going to do on the weekend, not what I was doing at school.

While I could talk in clear sentences — I represented the school in public speaking — I still had trouble reading and writing. In a year ten English class a teacher, walking around the classroom, looked over my shoulder at what I was writing and stopped. He picked up my book and read it out to the class. I was so embarrassed that I wagged English from that day on.

It was through my love for stunt work that I was given a book,

Bring on the Stunt Man by Ian Jamieson, who toured with Evel Knievel in 1979 and had appeared in Australian movies. That book — which I still have, held together by gaffer tape because I have worn it out — was like my Bible. I took it everywhere. I just looked at the pictures for the first couple of years but then I read it and re-read it. It's how I became a better reader and a better speller. If I haven't seen a word before it's hard for me to read. But, if I know it, I store it in my head. In primary school I had spelling tests, where we were given ten words to take home to learn. I would learn them, go back to school and ace it. If they took them out of order I wouldn't get one right.

When I was in year ten, a kid in year seven had funny coloured glasses. Other kids teased him about it. The glasses were for a problem like dyslexia. I wondered if they would have helped me but we had different problems: when he looked at words on a page they made a swirling pattern; when I saw them they looked right but arrived in my head back-to-front.

When I went back to school for year eleven the teachers said, 'What the hell are you doing here? We'd have thought you'd be the last person to come back.'

'That's a bit harsh,' I thought.

Everybody wanted to know what sort of job I was going to get. Stunt work obviously wasn't what people considered 'work' and I didn't know how to make money out of doing stunts in any case. So I went on to year eleven wanting to study physics, thinking eventually it would help with the stunts. There might actually be something I could learn from high school that would contribute to what I wanted to do.

'No Lawrence,' they said, 'you'll struggle. It's too hard for you.'

'Okay, fair enough. Can't I try though … ?'

'I think you'll have a lot of trouble.'

They talked me out of it.

I went through year eleven without the necessary drive or concentration and realised it would be ridiculous to go on to year twelve. The certificate wouldn't be worth anything. As adults we'd love to go back to school knowing what we know now. But I learned more watching the Discovery Channel than any time I spent at school.

Over the years my reading has improved remarkably. I can practically speed read — mainly because my mind recognises the first and last letter of each word and works it out from there. Significantly, my dyslexia has made me more determined. Now when anyone says 'You can't do it' or 'You won't do it' that just makes me think, 'Well you just sit there and watch me!'

Now there are friends from school and even people who weren't friends at school who come up and say hello. They tell me they let everyone know when they see me on television: 'I went to school with that kid!' They're amazed that (a) I'm still doing it and (b) I'm not dead.

Being different

I remember being in a newsagent's in 2007 when Evel Knievel died and an old guy I knew standing next to me said, 'I see your old mate died the other day.'

'Yeah, pretty sad isn't it?'

He said, 'When I first met you I knew there was something different about you, that you'd always do something different than everyone else.'

He was a member of the Lions Club, the community service organisation. My Dad was a member and they used to hold events at 'Monte Cristo'. He said he remembered me with a bow and arrow shooting at a bag full of hay, strung on a rope and swinging from a tree. 'Just from that,' he said, 'I knew you were after a challenge.'

The legendary Evel Knievel in Wagga Wagga, NSW (1979).

Dad (pictured with me at the Junee Showgrounds) was always there to lend a hand. He was my number one fan.

First day as Lawrence Legend, professionally. Dad and I talk about the first jump. (He would always say, 'If in doubt, go faster!')

I think that if you talked with anyone who has known me over the years they'd say I was always unconventional and thought outside the box. I presume I get that from my Dad because that's how he had to think.

I like to point out all the famous people who were dyslexic: actors, artists, scientists and athletes, including Thomas Edison, Albert Einstein, Leonard da Vinci, Pablo Picasso, a couple of American presidents and Formula One champion Jackie Stuart — all the famous people!

My dyslexia has had no bearing on my stunt work — though you might think left-right confusion could cause problems! But it's not so bad that I can't tell left and right. It's almost a Jekyll and Hyde situation as people prepare for a stunt. When you get on the bike you have a 'race face'. It's a whole different outlook, a whole different world when you become that person and you have to do that job.

As a kid I felt different when I got on a bike; like a superhero. Everything was colourful. I could see clearly what I wanted to do but often found it difficult to describe it and explain it to someone else. No-one could see it like I could see it.

My son and I are very spiritual people, like my Dad, connected in some way to the spirit world. I think my ability to know things about people and what will happen in the future has something to do with my dyslexia, something that makes me more connected to the energy of the world.

I have seen a saying in a Harley-Davidson dealership: Never ride faster than your guardian angel can fly. In my case it would be 'Never jump further ...'

In twenty-five years I had only two major accidents. There must be someone watching over me while I jump. I reckon my Dad's brother, whom I'm named after, is one of several guardian angels looking over my shoulder — I've known when I was going to crash and I've seen all my successful jumps, how they are going to end. If I thought it would be so bad I would die, I certainly wouldn't do it.

My Dad also reckoned there must be someone watching over me, especially financially. 'I don't know how you've pulled it off over the years. You've been down with no money in your pocket but if you've been determined enough and needed the money for something, you've found it.'

He used to say, 'I can't fault Lawrence for what he's doing. No matter if people think he's crazy or careless. He's exactly the same as me.'

My Dad grew up telling all of us, 'It doesn't matter, what you want to be in life. It doesn't matter if you want to be a doctor, a prostitute, a stunt rider, whatever; just try to be the best at it. That doesn't mean you *have* to be the best at it, just try to be the best at it.'

He said, 'You should be proud of whatever you do, no matter the reason. Everyone has a reason for doing something.'

We are all put on the earth for a reason. Mine might be to entertain people. Or there might be somewhere along the line where I discover what I am really here for.

When I see someone achieve something, whether it's a stunt performer or another sporting event, I get a huge chill up my spine. I get so excited for that person achieving greatness because I know what it is like to have those goals and dreams and how it feels when you achieve them. It comes down to respecting everyone else. Whether they want to be a hooker, or a doctor, a motorbike rider, a musician, a writer, whatever; you should respect that person's craft or ambition and say well done.

Whatever happens, I want to be a role model for children. My reward after a stunt is when a kid — or even an adult — comes up to me with wide eyes and says, 'That was absolutely amazing! That was so cool.'

My advice for kids going to school nowadays is to live your dreams, to not let anyone say you can't. There is no such thing as can't, there's only how you can do it. There's always a way around 'can't'. I used to go crook at my stepson. I'd ask him to do something and he'd say, 'I can't do that.' I'd tell him, 'There's no such word. You can do it. You mightn't be able to do it well, you might have trouble, but you can do it.'

All the naysayers and all the people who say can't do it and scoff at you, don't listen to them. The simple fact is if you want to do something bad enough, with drive and determination, there's nothing stopping you. Kids today are told they've got to be this, they've got to be that. They can be whatever they want. As long as they have the drive.

I sometimes think, though, that without the naysayers we wouldn't get anything done; we need them. I'm grateful for having them because they're the ones that push me harder.

4
Not Nine to Five

At sixteen and nine months I was allowed to attempt the learner's licence for my motorbike. I thought that was pretty good because I didn't have to have someone on the bike with me.

I failed.

I tried it on a mate's bike, a little 175 Yamaha two-stroke. The blinkers must have been put on as an afterthought because if you didn't rev the bike hard enough the indicators didn't work. The instructor came out the front of the Roads and Traffic Authority with me and had me do a couple of emergency stops. Then he sent me off on a figure eight course, where he couldn't see me. I was pretty sure if I came back in one piece he'd give me the licence.

He watched me go off but when I got to the first corner my indicator wasn't flashing because I didn't have the bike revved up enough. I lost four points straight away. As I came back the same thing happened: no indicators. Instantly eight points were gone and I didn't pass my licence.

I came back two weeks later, revving the bike so hard it sounded like it was being strangled. I did a wheel stand doing the figure eight in the back streets where the instructor couldn't see me but the blinkers worked.

I hardly rode on the road again for another ten years. But I had my licence.

When I went for my heavy rigid truck licence, so I could drive big box van trucks, the instructor hopped in the truck with me. My brother-in-law had come an hour earlier and given me some tips.

After I passed the knowledge test and was driving out the driveway the guy testing me said, 'Driving trucks must be easier than driving over them.'

He knew who I was.

I got that sinking feeling.

I failed the test because I couldn't see my blind spot in my mirrors while turning a corner and moved into the wrong lane. But the instructor didn't tell me and I did the same thing coming back. So I lost eight points. When I came back to take the test again the tester was a woman who didn't know me. I passed.

Kids that learn to drive on farms have a kind of defensive driving experience. There was a time before log books when you'd do the knowledge test, drive around a bit and do a test in an automatic. If you were in a country town there were no roundabouts or traffic lights. The hill start was probably a very low grade. It was so easy to get a licence that you really learned to drive on your provisional licence.

Today you can get discounts on your insurance if you do a defensive driving course. When I learned to two-wheel drive, the guy who helped me ran a defensive driving school. In Victoria, when you commit an offence, you can have the option of losing your licence or paying a smaller fine and doing a mandatory driving course. I think that's a brilliant idea.

People can teach you how to drive but few people learn how to drive defensively. I think everyone should have to do a basic course. In just a one-day course you can learn all you need to know about not getting yourself killed driving a car. And it should be mandatory to learn how to tow a trailer or caravan. It might sound strange coming from a daredevil, but I also think it's an enormous improvement nowadays that before you can get a motorbike licence you have to attend a course.

On four wheels

I had no difficulty passing my motor vehicle licence test. And I needed no instruction. I sat in the car once with Dad when I had my L's and he kept sliding across the seat.

'What are you doing that for?'

'You're driving too close to the line. I'm trying to get you to move over.' He thought he was a bit of a comedian.

I had plenty of practice, however. I'd spent a lot of time on my sister and brother-in-law's farm driving and I used to 'borrow' my Mum's car and go driving at night.

When my parents went out to dinner or a function I'd pinch the little Toyota Corolla, first asking what time they'd be home. I'd hop in the car and drive down to my mate's place, hang around for a bit and drive back again. That happened quite often but my parents never guessed why I was so interested in the time they'd be home. I even learned to reach under the dash and disconnect the speedo cable so they wouldn't suspect anything.

Eventually I got to picking my mates up and lapping around town. We were only fifteen or sixteen so I got them to wear hats so we looked older and wouldn't get pulled over by the police. We never did. It never occurred to me that my parents might see me driving around or that someone might see me and tell them.

One place we liked to go was a road out of Junee, the back way to Wagga Wagga, where there was a huge dip. It was fun to go through it quickly and make the car lift off its suspension. If you had a big run-up you could jump the car. My mates would get out and watch as I came around the corner and hit the dip. We measured my success by the number of posts in the guide rail I flew past. Unfortunately, the doors on Mum's poor old car wouldn't lock properly afterwards. Toyota Corollas are tough, though: you can't kill them. That's why I chose one for a two-wheeling car.

Once when I was doing the jump we saw a copper across the railway line watching us through binoculars. We jumped back in the car and hid at my mate's place for three hours, knowing the police would have to drive some distance to cross the railway line before they could start looking for us.

We'd been out on our excursions for six months or so when Mum and Dad went to town one night and I took three mates driving down a dirt road just out of Junee. I thought I'd try a handbrake turn but wasn't as skilled as I thought I was, hit the gutter and rolled the tyre off the rim. We were very lucky we didn't roll the car over. We jacked the car up and changed the tyre but I started to worry about how I was going to explain it or hide it.

When we hopped back into the car it wouldn't start. One of us had heard that if you pushed an automatic car up to thirty kilometres an hour you could roll start it. We pushed the Corolla up the big hill towards town and turned it around thinking we'd get the speed we needed going down the hill again. If we had any sense we would have pushed the car over the hill and it would have rolled back into Junee.

We got it up to thirty kilometres an hour, put the gears into drive and nothing happened. It came to a stop. We'd had enough of it and it was getting close to the time Mum and Dad would be home. I was going to have to confess to them. My mates disbanded to their separate houses and I phoned my sister who lived in town and told her what I'd done. I knew I'd be in trouble but I asked if she could come.

I was upset because I thought Dad was going to kill me. She called Mum and Dad and Dad came to get me. He gave me a bit of a lecture on the way home: What if someone got hurt? What if the police caught you and you got a record? He was pretty calm about it. I was probably harder on myself.

Dad said he always wondered why I wanted to know what time

they'd be home. Mum said I had to pay for the tyre and she demanded the keys to my motor bikes. She wouldn't believe that they didn't have keys. The only way I could appease her was to give her a bunch of keys from old cars in the shed.

It took some weeks before I was permitted to ride my bikes again. But when I got my provisional driver's licence I was allowed to drive that same car. I would still go down and pick up my mates. I was pretty well behaved. I wasn't one of those kids who looked for trouble. But if no-one was around I could handbrake the car into a parking spot in the main street.

I got into the most trouble doing handbrake turns in a dirt road near my friend Charlie Ford's place. I was banned from seeing Charlie after that. Mum said he was a bad influence. But it wasn't Charlie's fault. There were houses nearby where we were driving but it was pretty quiet so we'd practise handbrake turns and reverse flicks. We'd drive the car in reverse and suddenly spin the steering wheel really hard, which would force the car to flip around; as it flipped we'd put it back into drive, catch the steering wheel and drive off — ideally in one seamless action.

I'd seen it done in movies. I was teaching myself. I had no idea what I was doing. And I was doing it in Mum's car. But I had my licence, there was no-one around and I wasn't hurting anyone. My mates got out to see if I was cutting it around far enough.

Suddenly someone came out with a flashlight, 'Oi! What are you doin'?'

Everyone jumped back in the car and we drove off to another road where I continued practising. The road there wasn't wide, though, so I returned to our original spot, thinking we weren't making much noise and everyone would be asleep. But the guy with the flashlight came out again, only this time he took down the number on our licence plates.

A Honda CB360 twin, the bike I bought from my boss at Clark Rubber. It was the closest thing to Evel Knievel's Harley Davidson XR750.

Jumping ten cars at the Junee Show.

I dropped my mates off and went to bed. Dad came to my bedroom door: 'The police are here, they want to see you.' I knew full well what it was about.

We were in the front TV room and the copper there was known to be a 'notorious arsehole'. No-one liked him.

'We've got a report you were down doing skids and burnouts.'

'No, it wasn't me.'

The copper tried to tell us he'd done tests on the tread patterns, which was the biggest load of rubbish you'd ever heard. He was bluffing of course. He couldn't even find our front door in the dark, let alone the car in the back yard.

Six months later I got a notice saying I'd been charged with negligent driving. Dad was ropable because he believed me. And he was cranky at the cops.

We got a solicitor and the police found other witnesses who could identify the car. I had to fess up to Dad and the solicitor but I said I wasn't being reckless; I was just training. Dad was hugely disappointed in me.

By the time it went to court it had been a year since the actual event. I was then working at Clark Rubber and had a letter from my boss saying I needed my licence because I had to drive thirty or forty kilometres every day for work. My solicitor said I was training as a stuntman, I didn't think I was doing any harm and I had a booking to do a show at Sutton Forest. The judge said he should take my licence for public safety but that was pointless since I had been driving around for the past year. He said, 'I think you've learned your lesson. Don't be an idiot. Practise somewhere else.' He took six points off my licence and fined me a thousand dollars.

Ramping up

I left school at the end of 1987 and spent a year working in my Dad's pub, the Junee Hotel, doing the bookkeeping. Then I applied through an ad in a newspaper and got a job in sales at Clark Rubber, Wagga Wagga. Clark Rubber sold everything from futon lounges to pools. We sold pillows, wicker chairs, outdoor furniture and foam cut to size. I was young and pretty bulky so they thought I would be useful unloading the truck. I enjoyed it when I first started there — there was regular money coming in — but I found that I had a lot of time thinking about what I could be doing if I wasn't standing around waiting for customers. It's easier to be busy than it is to act busy. Some days I was just looking for things to do, dusting or rearranging gumboots.

Clark Rubber helped start my career as a daredevil, however, because my boss sold me the Honda CB360 twin — my first public appearance bike. The boss was a bike fanatic with old BSAs as well as the Honda. He said, 'I got this old bike. You might be interested.' He wasn't thinking I'd jump it. I don't think he really knew about my passion. I was trying to keep that quiet because I thought he wouldn't think it was responsible having someone working for him who might kill himself.

I went around to his place after work and bought the bike and a spare petrol tank for four hundred dollars. I thought, 'How cool would it be to jump this! No-one could think this big, heavy road bike could jump.' I mightn't have been too sure about jumping it myself but I imagined riding it with motocross handlebars and cut off exhausts. It would sound similar to a Harley — a big throbbing noise and a cackle when it came off acceleration.

I brought it home and built a small ramp, two feet off the ground, to see what it would do. To my surprise it didn't dive. It had a low centre of gravity and just flew naturally. So I built more ramps and did some practice jumps. And it still worked. I thought, 'This is it.

I'll jump these. This will get me noticed. Evel Knievel jumped big Harley-Davidsons and this is a big heavy bike. This will be cool. This is something different. Everyone else is jumping on motocross bikes.'

That's when I did some more research about Evel Knievel. I knew who he was but I had never seen any footage of him. We only had two television stations and our viewing was limited. I went to the library and took out a book, *Evel Knievel: The Cycle Jumper* by Marshall Spiegel. That got me interested in the showmanship and other aspects of his makeup. He was quite an interesting guy — take away the womanising and drinking and other things that went on. He grew up in a rough mining town in Montana in the United States, where some anti-social activities were perhaps more common than they are with kids today.

I have a documentary that tells of when he was a kid and a jewellery shop was robbed. He bought cheap costume jewellery from a store in a nearby town and came back and sold it to people who hoped they were picking up high end loot for a bargain.

It was the bike that got me interested in Evel Knievel rather than the other way around. I couldn't go ahead without knowing about my antecedents, understanding who'd kick-started the pursuit I loved. Most of the cycle jumpers I have spoken to don't seem to share my interest in the history; some fans do of course. But from those early library visits I now have bookcases full of books and newspaper clippings about stunt riders from all over the world.

In 1979 Evel Knievel toured Australia with Dale Buggins and Ian Jamieson. They came to Wagga Wagga, forty-five kilometres away, and I didn't know about it. People who were to shape my career were that close and I didn't get to see them. I saw nothing in the newspapers or on TV but kids at school were talking about it the day after.

Dale Buggins is one of Australia's most famous stunt motorcyclists. In 1978, aged seventeen, he jumped twenty-five cars with a Yamaha dirt bike, breaking a world record held by Evel Knievel. Dale then toured the United States and Australia in the Evel Knievel Spectacular but took his own life in Melbourne, in September 1981.

Ian Jamieson, stuntman and stunt coordinator, had a successful career in Australian film and television and, in 2014, aged sixty-one, was planning to set his sixth world record.

I have since spoken with Evel Knievel and with Dale Buggins' father and some of his team but I never met my heroes. Some people say you never should.

I went about building more makeshift ramps and made a half-decent costume. Twenty or thirty friends turned up one weekend and I did the jumps. We took a lot of good footage and thought, 'Wow!' I spoke to my Dad and said, 'Look, I'm serious. I need to build proper ramps; I can't be using these things. I'll try to get my first booking for a show.'

When I look back on my working life I have to acknowledge that, while I don't mind working, the whole nine to five thing bores me to tears. I don't know how people can do the same, repetitive thing day in and day out. When I left Clark Rubber I went to work for the paper shop next door. That lasted a week.

I was still at Clark Rubber when I made my first Lawrence Legend appearance. Every so often I'd see my old boss and he'd joke about selling me the old road bike that started it all. I was only with Clark Rubber for a year and a half and in that time I launched my career and jumped ten cars at Junee Show.

I'd left Clark Rubber by the time I broke my leg jumping fifteen cars in Wagga Wagga. I had one more job after that accident in 1991. It was for a bedding place. But after a week there I did a TV interview in my lunch break and the company's logo was in the background. They sacked me the next day because they didn't want to be associated with someone as reckless as me.

I think it was divine intervention. Someone was trying to tell me, 'You can try to have a normal job but we're not going to let you.'

5
THE LEGEND BEGINS

By the time I was in year ten and year eleven I was seriously thinking about a career in stunt work.

One day in the school library two girls from my class tried to talk me out of doing stunts for a living. They seemed concerned for me, as if they thought it was a death wish. That reaction — not understanding my motivation or commitment to my dream — is common. It might have looked risky to them but it was no different to parachuting or travelling to Africa to photograph wild animals. You could be killed; anything could happen.

It's a matter of perspective.

When people are concerned or interested about my work it's either because they care about what happens to me or because they don't care and want to see how bad things will turn out.

After school I had to figure out what I was going to do with my life. Dad got the Junee Hotel for a song and was going to keep it for a couple of years and sell it. But that meant a lot of work. I was roped into knocking down walls, rubbish removal and the bookkeeping.

After jumping Mum's car I eventually found a better bike; nothing crash hot but it meant I could start building ramps. Instead of using Mum's car I'd dig a hole, plant a piece of wood in the ground and hammer boards across it. At the beginning of 1989, when I was going to jump a road bike, the take-off ramp was welded together and quite good but the landing ramp was made the old way: built out of the ground using timber slats and whatever else I could find. I couldn't afford anything better.

Although my parents didn't discourage me from stunt work, their attitude was, 'Well that's great but what are you going to do about a job? You can't just rely on that.' They wouldn't fund the motorbikes because they didn't want to be responsible for me hurting myself. But they couldn't talk me out of it.

When I went to Dad later in 1989, I said, 'You all think it is a bit of joke. You don't think I'm serious but I really need your help. I need a bit of capital to build the ramps.' It was a serious conversation and after that Dad bent over backwards to help me. It was like I had to make a bit of a speech. I don't think Mum changed her attitude but it certainly changed Dad's. He thought, 'Well obviously he is very determined; this is what he wants to do. I'll do my best to help him.' And ever since then he did.

Occasionally Dad would say to someone who was close to me, 'Can you keep an eye on Lawrence; I'm worried he's not going to take the time to set it up properly.' He never really had to worry.

Mum's gone along with it for the simple fact there is not much she can do but worry about my safety. She used to be a nervous wreck because she didn't see the planning and practice, everything that goes into a jump; she only saw what was in the papers, what was on television, how dangerous it was. 'My God! There's no way he's going to survive this.'

But a lot of it is showmanship. It's the illusion of making something a lot more dangerous than it actually is. For instance, in the Wall of Fire — poles with planks between them, doused in fuel — I do a wheelie and break through it. Everyone thinks it's fantastic. I would prefer to take it out but everyone loves it so much I have to do it. It's the allure of fire.

What people perceive as dangerous and what actually is dangerous are quite different. Often people are less impressed by the seriously dangerous stunts than by stunts that are dramatic but very safe.

The difference between danger and safety comes down to practice, trial and error, and an element of luck. From the beginning, with no-one to teach me, it was trial and error. I didn't attend motorbike races and few friends rode motorbikes. If it worked the first time and I didn't hurt myself, I must have done something right.

I learned very quickly with each step. If I did six jumps in one day, on the sixth jump I'd have learned a lot about how the bike reacted and how the ramp worked. I also learned how much luck played a part. A daredevil relies on a combination of luck, guts and determination. If I believe I can do it there's nothing stopping me. It doesn't matter how bad the set up is, I can do it. But if I start thinking about it or friends and family come up saying they're not happy about it or it doesn't look right, then I begin to doubt. The only time I've had accidents is when I've doubted myself.

Accidents are part of the learning process. You need them to make sure you understand that you are not indestructible.

Appearance counts

Part of the theatre of a stunt is the costumes. I had my whole outfit worked out by the time I turned professional in 1989. It hasn't differed much over the years because you shouldn't change your brand if you want people to recognise it and remember it.

I wanted to give a new lease of life to black leathers; not something that was dark and evil, but tough nevertheless. An early outfit, before I became professional, was a black jacket with red sewn onto it but it didn't look right. So I went to blue with white stars and eventually to a white stripe with a blue centre and white stars to bring out the stripes. I learned you have to allow for the audience watching and for photographs being taken. You need to be able to stand out. If you are too dark you'll be lost in the night.

Since Dad was a tailor, he sewed the stripes onto my leather jackets

— I couldn't afford custom leathers. I only ever had one set of leather pants because I didn't like their movement. I went for black Levi's jeans with a stripe sewn down the outside seam. I figured if I had an accident they would cut them off me, so I wasn't going to pay a fortune for leathers. That was before motocross gear came out with lightweight polyester fabric. The denim was durable. I wore knee braces underneath and boots up to the top of my calves, so very little was unprotected. People ask why I don't have more padding. For the stunts I do the padding would only stop some bruising. It certainly wouldn't stop a broken arm or leg.

I also wanted something with a bit of class, something no-one had tried before. I'd seen someone jump in a bow tie but thought that wasn't typically Australian. For most people I knew a shirt and tie was more usual formal wear. On a bike it made people look twice. When they saw me first they would think I was the manager or promoter — until I hopped on the bike. Then, 'Hang on. Where's the tattooed, bearded bikie guy who is going to do the stunt?'

That was what I was trying to get away from. Many of the stunt drivers I had seen were show or carnival folk who lived a day-to-day existence. They did it hard, living out of a trailer or camper van. I wanted to be totally opposite to that, something that got people's attention, following Evel Knievel's template of a cross between Liberace and Elvis Presley or Las Vegas entertainers Siegfried & Roy. There had to be a degree of showmanship. When people asked why I wore the shirt and tie I would joke, 'Well, if anything really bad happens, wherever I land all they have to do is dig a hole next to me and roll me in. I'm dressed for the occasion.'

The name Lawrence Legend was one of several options, including Lawrence Dare. But I thought lots of famous people, from Mickey Mouse to Marilyn Monroe, had alliteration in their names, so I looked through the dictionary to find something beginning with L to pair with Lawrence. Legend came up quickly. That was before the popularity of the phrase 'You're a legend', otherwise I wouldn't have chosen it. I thought Legend would eventually be accepted and recognised simply as a name. I am still annoyed when people call me Lawrence *the* Legend.

The Australian flag usually featured in the act. It was partly showmanship and the similarity of the colour scheme, but I am certainly proud to be Australian. A lot of our focus was on the American market and how much they loved Australians. Sometimes when I see how patriotic Americans are I wonder why we can't be like that. We need to be a little bit more proud of our country.

My first professional jump in July 1989 was on a freezing cold morning at 'Monte Cristo'. We had to get the ramps together before the news cameras and reporters arrived. It took a good couple of hours to assemble. We were still putting it together when they turned up. I had to go and get changed. None of my friends knew I would be wearing a shirt and tie under my jacket. When I came down their reaction was amusing. They had big smiles on the faces, thinking it was over the top. But they knew about my theatrical side.

I have a great photograph of my Dad standing next to me while I am on the bike; a sentimental pairing with the photo of Dad beside me when I was a few months old sitting on the penny-farthing. Dad was supportive from that day, always encouraging me to go faster, not slower. He paid to have someone fabricate the ramp sections that two mates and I welded together when I got home from Clark Rubber, down in the shed from seven until midnight. The first time I put the take off ramp together one of my mates said, 'You're going to kill yourself for sure. That ramp is huge. There is no way you're going to bloody survive launching off that.' The design of the ramp was just what I thought was right. I didn't struggle with it. It seemed to come natural to me.

I jumped seven cars that day because that was how many we could

Nose-down landing with no safety deck over the last car (1989). It was so close to a crash and over the handle bars.

First jumps as Lawrence Legend for the news cameras (1989).

The jump that ruptured my kidneys. I came up short. Notice the cameraman between the cars. This is why there is no footage of this crash.

find: my Mum and Dad's car, my friends' cars, anything. The cars were spaced far enough apart for the doors to open so my friends could get their belongings from them. They were confident — or trusted in my confidence — that I wouldn't land on them.

The first jump is always nerve wracking; it's horrible to do. You can do them over and over again after that; they are a lot easier. But the first one is the trial and error jump. A million things can go wrong: a bad take off, a bad run, having second thoughts, mechanical failure. When you do it and make it look easy people say, 'I could have done that.' But if you make a mistake they say, 'You're braver than me, I wouldn't have done that.'

That day I did three jumps successfully. Before I attempted the fourth a cameraman climbed under the ramp to shoot from a different angle. I came up short (and the cameraman missed the shot). The ramp was steep and I was overconfident. When the front wheel of the bike hit, it loaded the suspension and as I went up the ramp the bike did a wheel stand and lost speed. I didn't have a safety deck — a platform covering the last couple of cars to stop the back wheel catching the top of the ramp — so the bike jammed suddenly and the handlebars turned sideways into my stomach and threw me over. That's how I ruptured my kidneys.

Over twenty-five years I've had very few accidents. It's pretty incredible. None of the accidents scared me. As soon as you have an accident the first thing you do is assess what you've hurt. You lie there and think what you can't feel or do. I've never had the fear of realising I couldn't feel my legs or arms. It was just, 'I've fallen off. What damage have I done?'

The first accident just felt like I'd been winded really badly. I had no idea I'd ruptured my kidneys. My mate's father, an ambulance driver, was there for the stunt and told me if I started passing blood to get straight to a doctor. But we didn't think much more of it. I was actually coming good. It was sore but the bruising hadn't started. I'd finished packing up the ramps and we had lunch at 'Monte Cristo' and watched a video of the jump. It wasn't until that afternoon when I went to the toilet and I was passing blood mixed with urine ... and there was a lot ... and it was very dark ... that it scared the hell out of me.

One of my mates drove me to the doctor. He loaded me into an ambulance, sent me straight to hospital and said I shouldn't be moving around at all. I spent a few days in hospital and it was another two weeks until I was back on a bike. I was sore and sorry for a month afterwards but still working at Clark Rubber.

When I broke my ankle two years later I was back on a bike before my cast was off.

I didn't practise much between the jump at 'Monte Cristo' and jumping ten cars for my first live audience at the Junee Show in October. I knew what I had to do. It was only a few more cars. I brought the ramp heights down and added a safety deck. I didn't have to jump as high and it worked perfectly.

My change room for the Junee Show jump was the back of a horse float. It was one of Dad's home-made horse floats that we used to bring the ramps to the showground. It smelled. As I was coming out I smacked my head on the door and one of my good friends sad, 'Oh God, if this is how the day starts we've got no hope.'

Three days before the show the local Honda shop loaned me a CR500 to use for wheelies. I hadn't ridden a bike that powerful before. I thought, 'It's just a bike; I'll work it out.' I picked it up one afternoon after work and brought it home. With two mates to help, I quickly got it off the back of my ute. Still in my suit pants, short-sleeved business shirt and tie, I jumped on the bike, put on my helmet and rode up the hill wheel-standing, thinking, 'Oh, this bike goes!'

The road was steep and gravelly, however, and when I turned around to go back I flipped the bike. I slid along the ground watching someone else's bike doing cartwheels down the road. My hands dragged along the gravel as I tried to get up to chase the bike. That was my only concern. It took all the skin off the palms of my hands and my forearms. My mates had hopped in the ute and were driving up to see what all the dust and noise was about. I bent the bike up and never got to use it but had to pay to get the handlebars fixed.

Three days later, stiff as a board and with my hands bandaged, I stepped out of the float and banged my head. 'That's two bad things,' I thought, wondering what the third would be. I didn't have to wonder long. After I landed the jump I was so excited I had my hands off the bike and in the air. I flew around the corner and had to dive on the brakes to avoid colliding with another horse float.

After a jump there's time to reflect. I have wondered if it's like a woman after childbirth: 'I'll never do that again.' But not long after they say they'd do it again in a heartbeat, it's such a wonderful thing.

Sometimes it's like that for me. 'That scared the hell out of me. I'll never do it again.' There's an adrenalin rush then a huge wave of release. Sometimes it seems as if the pressure of having to do the stunt — because that's what you've promised, that's the agreement — is more of a problem than the stunt itself. But all the trouble you had getting to that point seems to be gone when the jump is complete; all the drama of setting up, negotiating with promoters and show society people, that all goes out the window. And, added to the relief and satisfaction, you're thinking, 'Great, I can get paid now.'

It went quiet media-wise after the launch in July. Knowing what I know now there would have been more media hype leading up to the Junee Show jump. I just spoke to a few people. I didn't even issue a press release. Things have changed since then.

My early relationships with the media were very informal and certainly not strategic. I just accepted invitations on the front of the newspaper for people to submit stories.

The very first article, about my first professional attempt to jump ten cars at Sutton Farm at Moss Vale, was written by a girl I went to school with. She came to my tenth birthday party and I hit her in the head with a rock during a 'shot put' competition. She just happened to be the one who wrote the story.

When she came with a photographer to do the interview for the story I was on my lunch break from Clark Rubber. The photographer wanted me to smile more so said, 'Imagine she has no clothes on.' I pulled a face, thinking, 'Hang on, I went to school with the girl. I don't want to think of her like that.' But that's the photo that appeared in the newspaper.

I started out quite naïve. I wasn't aware of the importance of protecting my image. I was also serious about my career and very reserved when talking about it to people — especially the media. Later, when I joined the Toyota V6 HiLux Heroes, I received media training and learned you have to be bubbly and outgoing, within reason; more flamboyant and outspoken. Some of it I had picked up along the way but it still provided a valuable insight into the way the media works and how interviews are conducted. Sometimes the news is highly controlled and the stories finely constructed; at other times I have sent in press releases and they have appeared word for word.

I now understand what to say and what not to say. I know how words can be twisted. I am cautious while being more vocal than I was in the early days. I didn't need to be as cautious then. The media treated me pretty well and there was less negativity than there is today. The newspapers were written and edited locally and it wasn't as harsh or sensationalised. Now there's always a reminder of the need to be careful.

A reporter called recently following up on the progress of the Stuntman and Daredevil Hall of Fame. When I mentioned the growing collection of stunt cars and motor bikes I said it would be like an auto-museum. The next day the paper said, 'Legend deviates from DA approval'. I had to make sure council understood I wasn't changing anything.

I haven't had any really bad experiences with the media. But still I trust them as far as I can throw them. I think that's a wise thing. If you get too relaxed with them they'll bite you on the backside. At the same time, you need to keep them onside.

I'm always amazed about what journalists think is a story and what's not a story. Sometimes I have made world record jumps and the local papers haven't printed anything. One newsreader I knew well sent back a press release questioning the authenticity of one of my world records because I had set so many.

I've done some amazing stunts, jumped over fifteen trucks on my motorcycle and done Tunnels of Fire, but if I jump a silly old double decker bus over a row of motor cycles people think that's the best thing — it gets two-page spreads in UK magazines and news reports all round the world.

Jumping a bus had its own dangers and was entertaining but it was also a bit embarrassing. It changed my thinking about chasing difficult records — I needed to jump over unconventional and unlikely things. That's what the public, Guinness World Records, and the TV news producers want to see. If you are like everyone else you're just another in the long line of daredevils.

I've been interviewed by some famous journalists and well-known personalities — Rove McManus, George Negus, Warwick Moss and Grant Denyer — but I think they put their pants on the same way as everyone else. They are just people doing an interview.

When we had breakfast radio show hosts Kyle Sandilands and Jackie O down to do a story on 'Monte Cristo' and I gave Kyle one of the Lawrence Legend kids books he said, 'I think I've heard of you somewhere before.' It's funny how many people say that.

My eldest sister brought my young nephews to see my seven-car jump at 'Monte Cristo'. She had been to a medium and was warned that I would have an accident but didn't tell me that. A journalist had spoken to her and I read it in the newspaper later.

I was confident that day. At my happiest. I knew that was where I wanted to be and I was doing what I wanted to do.

6

CRASH HEARD AROUND THE WORLD

I worked with my support team toward the 1991 jump in Wagga Wagga. First with six cars, then seven. Then the Junee show in 1989 with ten cars. The plan was to do fifteen then twenty. That would break Evel Knievel's record. From fifteen to twenty didn't seem that much when you said it quickly.

We knew how much more speed we'd need to get there. I was perhaps naïve trying to land on the small landing ramp. Coming up short or long would result in the same thing. Going long the bike would buckle and buck me off. We had to be precise. The only problem with jumping ramp-to-ramp is you must rely on your gut feeling or a speedometer. The 1991 jump was one of the few times I used a speedometer because I thought more often than not they muck you up. Your gut feeling is more accurate.

That year I had an association with the Hillis Ford dealership and they got me a job at Wagga Wagga's Gumi Festival, which featured a race down the Murrumbidgee River on inflated inner tubes. We arranged with the festival organisers to use Bolton Park, a big park in the centre of Wagga Wagga, and the Ford dealer provided some second hand cars.

On the day of the jump the ground was very wet because they had the sprinkler system on the night before. The ground was mushy but not too bad. I could get a good run-up and attain the speed I needed.

We put the fifteen cars and ramps in place and between three and five thousand people turned up. It was a huge crowd. The event was free and had been well advertised. The jump was around three in the afternoon and people came down for a look; they probably thought I wouldn't make it.

The Mayor of Wagga Wagga, my old principal, was there. In addition to the local press and TV station there was a photographer from the *Australasian Post* magazine. The local TV news anchor was the announcer. I did three run-bys on the CB360 and I thought it was looking good. The test runs were more about psyching myself up than getting the crowd excited. Someone should have lynched me for not just doing the jump.

I didn't know it at the time but at the far end some police were using their radar to clock my speed. They registered my run-bys as being the speed I needed — ninety-seven kilometres an hour. But when I did the jump I was going five kilometres an hour slower. I landed a car-length short, with my back wheel catching the end of the safety deck. It stopped the bike and threw the front end down, with the wheel crashing through the deck. I was catapulted off the bike.

I flew through the air thinking, 'I haven't hit the ground yet.' My body was flipping in what seemed like slow motion. Suddenly there was a hard thud and another flip and I was on the ground. My first thought was that someone must have captured that on camera; we'd set up angles from every direction. When my crew ran over to me in their 'Lawrence Legend' shirts, one of my mates asked if I was all right.

'No. I've broken something.'

I wasn't concerned. I didn't have laboured breathing and wasn't feeling dizzy. The ambulance was soon on its way. I knew I'd done some damage but I just lay there and let them do their job. I could hear the crowd, all the noise and excitement.

Looking back at the footage of the jump you can hear the gasp as I hit the ramp and crashed and then it's just dead silence. They saw me airborne. They saw me hit the ground with my left foot. They saw my leg penetrate the earth, ankle deep. They saw my body coil into a ball and then continue over, snapping the ankle. It sounds terrible but I wonder if my ankle digging into the ground in fact cushioned my landing and prevented even more severe damage. As it was, I'd also fractured my back, though not seriously.

The good thing about the accident was that I didn't have to pack up the gear. I had good friends to help with that.

The road to recovery

I don't think it was an issue of negligence — just an attitude among health professionals at the time — but if you went to hospital with a self-inflicted injury the doctors and nurses weren't very attentive. It was almost as if, 'It's your own stupid fault; we have more important cases to deal with.' I didn't have any painkillers for two and a half hours after the accident. While I was in emergency a doctor examining me moved my foot from side to side, I suppose to see how broken my ankle was. It hurt like all hell and I nearly passed out. He dropped my foot and wandered off. He came back with another doctor, picked my leg up and did the same thing. The pain was unbearable. When he returned again I said, 'If you do that one more time there's going to be trouble.'

During the accident I collided heavily into the metal fuel tank on the bike, making a significant dent and ripping my leathers in the groin and cutting one of my testicles. It was just a scratch but I thought the doctor examining my old fella could have been a bit less blasé.

It took two days before they operated on my ankle. They put a metal pin through it to stop it moving and a plate with screws along the side to repair the bone and keep it in place.

I gained some perspective on my situation, however, because I was sharing a ward with another patient who had a motorbike accident in the bush. He had an injury similar to mine but also shattered his other

The Bolton Park jump (1991) when I only managed to clear 14 of the 15 cars.

Fractured back and broken left ankle. This jump made me famous.

Publicity shot with Honda CB360.

leg, which had an array of nuts and bolts on the outside holding it together. The poor guy would cry at night and sing out because he was in so much pain.

I was out of hospital in less than a week, with a cast on my leg that looked horrible because I had bled into it. My back was sore and I was bruised all over and couldn't lie down properly. I wanted to get up and see how much damage I had done to the bike. I could use crutches but as soon as I stood up the blood would rush to my ankle, which would swell and press onto the cast. When I went back to hospital they cut the cast so it could expand with my ankle. But then it was so loose my leg twisted inside it, causing more pain. I went back again to get a new cast, pointing out that the old one was beginning to stink. But the doctor, about to go on his lunch break, just taped it up.

After six weeks I returned to the hospital so they could take the long pin out of my ankle joint. A year later they were to remove the metal plate. I told my friends to feel the screws beneath the surface of my skin. It felt creepy. When the year was up I went to the family doctor, who told me to make an appointment to get the plate out. When I saw the surgeon he told me they had taken the plate out when they removed the pin, eleven months earlier. I felt like an idiot because I'd been telling people they could feel the screws. In that case, I asked the surgeon, would I be right to jump motorbikes again. He gave me a puzzled look and said, 'I suppose so.'

When I went home I examined my leg and thought, 'I can feel those screws. I am sure they're in there.' So I went to see my local doctor who had less than complimentary things to say about the surgeon. We had some x-rays taken and took them to the surgeon. It turned out there had been a patient before me with the same injury and the same plate in his ankle ... and the same surname. I had been confused with someone else.

Some reporters spoke to me while I was in hospital immediately after the accident and I made the news in the paper and on local television. But I also made the *National Enquirer* in America, all the Australian metropolitan dailies, and newspaper and TV news worldwide. Within six months TV shows were calling asking to buy the footage for their 'stunts gone wrong' programs. I've since sold dozens of packages like that. When I was first offered a few hundred dollars I thought that was pretty good. Now I'd be looking at a minimum of fifteen hundred dollars. Some would pay a lot more.

I didn't make any money at the time but people are still interested in the footage today. It's almost as if you can't have a stunt career unless you have had an accident you can use to show how dangerous what you do is. I don't want to do it again but I wouldn't take it back either. It was spectacular and Evel Knievelesque.

Accidents can happen of course, no matter what you do. A lot of my jumps are close-quarters jumps, where there is no landing room; for instance, where I jump trains and run into a wall. The 'accident' at the end is controlled.

When I crashed the bike it forced the safety platform down and smashed the windows out of the last two cars. I still have a few pieces of glass that a mate was quick to collect for me. He said after the jump there was not a piece of glass to be picked up: all the small crystal pieces from the broken safety glass in two windscreens had been souvenired. Along with the flags and signage from the ramps.

The Ford dealer sold one of the cars within a week of the accident … because I hit it.

When I tell bike people I did that jump on a Honda CB360 twin their eyes widen: 'Really? That thing? They weren't good enough to ride on the road, let alone fly through the air!' While I was in hospital I knew it would be some time before I'd jump a big bike again. But I had done what I had set out to do: get people's attention. I could go back to motocross bikes. They were more forgiving and didn't need down ramps. The CB360 had done its job.

The bike was no use for jumping after that but I used it to break some records in the Tunnel of Fire. It was good for that because it had big cardboard cartridge air filters on the side that held a lot of air. When you do the Tunnels of Fire, oxygen is drawn from their centre as the fire burns. People have been killed attempting the Tunnel of Fire on bikes with smaller air filters because they'd get halfway through and suddenly there was no oxygen and they stopped.

Even though fire scares me I still have a fascination for it.

I got my pyrotechnic's licence in 1991. All the TV shows had pyrotechnics exploding. I thought if I had a licence I could do that myself.

I first went to do an explosives course that you need for mining. Four weeks in I was told I really just needed a pyrotechnics licence. But that meant I had to be working on a movie set under the supervision of another pyrotechnic for twelve months. I was living in Junee. We don't make many movies in Junee. And I didn't know anyone in the movie business and I didn't have the time to wait for a year.

During a show I met people from Howard and Sons Fireworks, a well known family-owned business in Sydney. One guy took a shine to me and wrote me a reference. I got another reference from a pyrotechnics expert and soon had a licence of my own.

Since the terrorist attacks in the United States on September 11, 2001, it is much harder and much more expensive.

When I did the jump again in 2000 I also used cars from Hillis Ford. This time they were all the same model, which looked much more professional. The ground was bigger still and the jump was on a different scale. It was higher and longer and I was on a modern motocross bike. People thought it was fantastic. It was nowhere near the furthest jump that anyone had done and not the most cars ever jumped. It was just me coming back.

My stunt work had been very quiet up until that accident in 1991. I was taking it seriously but still hadn't figured out how to make a living out of it. Everything spiralled slowly upwards after the accident. And it wasn't until 1996 with my first big Australian record jump that things took off.

7
It's Stunt Business

In 1993 at Canberra Speedway I met Johnny 'Wonder' Fogwell, who began his professional career in 1971 and in his time had broken many distance records. I went up to him, introduced myself, had my picture taken with him and chatted about the stunt business.

About a week after that he phoned me. He was trying to sell me Dale Buggins' old highwire bike. Johnny had bought it from Ken Buggins, Dale's father, after Dale had died. Johnny had used it for many years himself.

Of course I was interested because it had belonged to Dale Buggins and I was already thinking of building a museum to preserve the memories of stunt performers and daredevils. Johnny wanted around seven thousand dollars — much more than I could afford — but I said I was interested. He sent photographs and we talked about it. I tried to figure out a way I could use it myself to help pay for it.

A few months went by and I decided to move to Queensland, where Johnny lived, to see if I could get into the movie industry. Johnny himself had done some film work — from TV shows to films like *Mission Impossible* and *Coolangatta Gold*. He lived near the Gold Coast in Tambourine Mountains. I moved up there so he could train me to use the highwire bike before I bought it and so I could hand my resume in to Warner Bros. Movie World. The employment pathway at the time was to start with the Police Academy Stunt Show and from there you might get a chance to work in movies.

I was just a kid from the country. My stunts were self-taught. I had no idea what I was getting myself into.

While I waited to hear from Movie World I got a job in a motorbike shop. You name it, I did it: pushed motorbikes, cleaned motorbikes, sold motorbikes, delivered motorbikes. When I learned I could try out for the Stunt Show, I visited Johnny and asked for some tips. He mainly showed me fighting scenes, which didn't interest me. I wanted to know about cars and bikes.

The coordinator at the Stunt Show knew I was a bike guy but wanted to test my 'falling off scaffolding' skills, first climbing clumsily (as in a slapstick, comedy routine) and then more seriously. The scaffolding was three storeys high. I joked that I wouldn't have to act clumsy but did the clumsy climb and then went up again as fast as I could.

The next step was high falls. We went out the back to a tower with a high fall pad. I had done falls before but only falling sideways before landing on my back, not the forward tuck, going headfirst, tucking at the last minute and landing on my back. The stunt coordinator sent me to the first level, where I did a side drop. He said that wouldn't be any good, would I feel confident doing a forward drop? I said I'd never done one. He sent me to the second level but then changed his mind and instead put me on a bike and got me to do wheel stands in the back lot.

It was a two-stroke bike. In my shows I did power wheel stands, on the throttle with plenty of room. I was racing from one end to another until Batman parked his Batmobile, got out and walked across my path. His cowl was rigid so he couldn't turn his head to see the imminent danger. I nearly wiped out Batman!

After I screeched to a halt I noticed the other stunt performers had been watching me. Most weren't the bike stunt type. They were muscle-bound acrobats and blonde girls in tank tops.

The stunt coordinator said my wheel stands were too fast for the spot they had. I said I could slow it down but the bike wasn't good for that. Nevertheless, he said, that was the bike I had to learn on. Then he took me to the cars, Chevrolet Caprices — big tanks. He wanted me to take one down the end of the arena and do a handbrake turn.

'Where's the handbrake?'

'Well, we don't use an actual handbrake. There's a switch on the floor that separates the front wheel brakes from the back wheel brakes, so, when you get to the end, jump on the brakes as hard as you can and that will lock up only the back wheels and make the car do a one-hundred and eighty degree turn.'

I'd done a million handbrake turns but never like that. And never in a left-hand drive car.

I raced to the end but because I didn't jump hard enough on the brakes the car didn't spin around properly. He gave me another chance but it still didn't spin around properly. Then he gave a tip: 'Put your foot flat on the gas when you take off; three-quarters of the way down you'll see a white mark on the concrete; when you get to that, turn the wheel ninety degrees and jump on the brakes as hard as you can. I guarantee you'll spin around on the same spot every time.'

That's what happened. There was no skill involved. You just had to follow instructions when you got to the markings.

Next I had to fall off a roof, onto an awning and make it look like I hit my head on the way down. That was fun.

Then I had to speak lines from the show. Another guy was trying out with me. I discovered later he didn't have stunt experience but used to sell popcorn at the show, so he knew the lines in script — which we had to speak in an American accent. As theatrical as I am, I had never tried that before. I came across like a drunken Irishman. The popcorn guy, however, had been there four years listening to the routine and nailed it perfectly.

Guess who got the job?

It was easier to train him to spin a car than it was to train me to speak with an American accent.

In the six months I was there I saw some big-budget live stunt shows and a guy who I'd seen before at the Summernats in Canberra; I gained some experience and made some contacts.

I also heard about several people who were injured on movie sets. The accidents included one guy missing a fall pad and hitting his head, one falling from a helicopter onto moving water, and another burnt when running from a tunnel as it exploded. When aspiring stunt people were needed for movies being filmed in a lot adjacent to Warners Brothers Movie World they approached the Police Academy Stunt Show. Even if the stunt people had been at the Stunt Show for a while and were confident, they knew only the falls and other stunts used in the show. If they were asked to do a stunt like fleeing a burning tunnel they couldn't turn the job down because there would be three other people from the Stunt Show who'd give it a go. They wouldn't even know what questions to ask about how the pyrotechnics were being managed. Inexperienced people were taking foolish risks.

The big screen

It became clear that getting a job in the movie industry was more about who you knew rather than what you knew. You had to be in with the stunt coordinator. I was disillusioned. I thought the whole setup would be much more professional. It was a primitive time for the stunt industry in the movies. A lot of leading stunt coordinators were people like me who were self-taught, using basic equipment, and learning on the job. Johnny told me about a stunt coordinator whose brother was a famous racing driver. While shooting a movie he was supposed to hit a tree stump and roll a car onto its roof. Johnny was strapping him in and the stunt coordinator told him he had never rolled a car before.

I thought I would be better off with regular work doing stunt shows in New South Wales than having to hold down several jobs while waiting for an occasional movie role on the Gold Coast.

As the industry grew, stunt performers were required to be union members, hold stunt performers cards and be assessed by a board of their peers. Now it is easier for stunt people like me because if the production houses can't find someone in their crew for a stunt that is less common, for instance two-wheeling, they can bring in outsiders as specialised performers. But it's still pretty cut throat. There's not a lot of work for people who do movie stunts. And there's a high turnover because it's so hard to make a living.

Sometimes it helps if a stunt performer can act a bit because then they can secure small roles where their faces don't need to be obscured as they would if they were standing in for a 'real' actor. There has been a long history of crossover between actors and stunt performers; ever since the silent era with Buster Keaton and Harold Lloyd, right up to modern times, especially with martial arts performers like Jackie Chan. The big stars, though, can't do their own stunts because it's such an insurance risk.

There are people who have the drive to be actors; who will do anything to appear on stage and screen. What I do is entertainment; it's acting to a degree. But being in stunt work is probably not the best way to break into the acting business.

I still had some opportunities to participate in the filming of stunts. One was a commercial for Holden Captiva, where the Captiva drove across the skyline of Sydney, jumping from one skyscraper to the next. They asked me to provide the ramps. I had some old ramps but built new ones because they were paying decent money. They said they didn't need me to jump, just the ramps, because they had a stunt team.

They first set up the ramps on the top level of the Sydney Entertainment Centre car park. While I wasn't driving, I went along to see how they used the ramps. They took some shots but there wasn't enough room to do the actual jump.

The late and great Dale Buggins, Wagga Wagga, NSW (1979).

One of the three double-decker bus jumps over bikes I made at the Summernats Car Festival in 2004.

Crashing into the side of a van on purpose: the human catapult stunt (2004).

Jumping over trains was one of my favourite stunts (1997).

Their stunt driver had his head out the window to make sure he was lined up as he approached the ramp. There was even a piece of wood screwed onto the ramp so he couldn't veer off line. Another guy was giving him directions and they had a pole in the centre for further guidance. I thought, 'If you can't drive in a straight line up a ramp, you've got problems.'

Then they hired the ramp for another week and moved it to the car park at Olympic Park in western Sydney. After some practice jumping they decided they couldn't land on my eight-foot wide landing ramp, so extended it two feet each side, with scaffolding and planks.

The take off ramp was two single tracks with nothing between them. They thought that was dangerous (although if they were driving up the ramp they didn't need anything between them; if one wheel went into the middle the other wheel wasn't on the ramp at all and they hadn't gone up the ramp). They said there was no way they could drive up the ramp at sixty kilometres an hour. I said I drove up it at seventy kilometres an hour in a car whose wheels were wider than the track.

The stunt guys figured out I knew what I was talking about. They wanted to copy my ramp design because they were only used to old-fashion wedge ramps that jolted the car. And they wanted me to teach them two-wheel driving.

They were jumping a Captiva and an Opal, which they jumped too far down the landing ramp because they weren't used to jumping that distance; again, saying they knew how to do it but only working it out after they got the job. It was mind boggling that they employed five guys to do that. But they say when you make movies that are commercial it is hurry up and wait. You stand around all day for five minutes of filming. I'd almost prefer to work on a low budget movie where they have to keep going because they don't have the luxury for twenty takes.

Today a lot of movie action is computer-generated imagery (CGI), which makes it harder for people doing live stunts because the audience expects to see a car cartwheel five times, bounce off a wall, land on its wheels and drive away. And, while the action sequences using technological advances result in safer working conditions for stunt performers, they will have fewer opportunities to work.

All this change could turn out to benefit traditional stunt performers. It provides an opportunity for people of my generation to take their kids to live shows so they can see how it used to be done. It's a good time for me to be passing on the torch. If I wait another ten years everything will be computer generated; nothing will be live-action stunts. And the younger generation of stunt performers will have even less idea how stunts are really done.

While the movies may not be for me professionally, I still have an enormous interest in them and how stunts have been performed through past decades. For instance, in old westerns they used to trip up horses (and don't anymore); they modified stirrups and saddles so stuntmen could fall off horses or jump from a horse to a carriage more easily.

Some of my favourite movies with action scenes include *The Blues Brothers*, which has a lot of car stunts, and the original *Gone in 60 Seconds*. Its follow-up, *The Junk Man,* also had lots of car stunts. Back when we had VHS tapes I'd hire movies and record just the stunt scenes. They'd just get me thinking about other stunts that would look good in movies. I've even thought about a script that would make the Guinness Book of Records for most continuous stunts in a movie.

I'd love to meet Zoe Bell, the New Zealand actress and stuntwoman who doubled for Lucy Lawless on *Xena: Warrior Princess* and for Uma Thurman in *Kill Bill* and even played herself in Quentin Tarantino's film, *Death Proof*. I admire Tarantino's outlook and interest in stunt performers. And he's a fan of action films. I really like *Death Proof* — the second half at least because that's where all the action is. But sometimes I think I could make the stunts even *more* exciting.

I suspect it is only stunt performers like me who pay attention to the stunt credits at the end of movies. I'm always curious about how the good stunts are performed. In *Terminator II*, with Arnold Schwarzenegger, there's a shot where a Harley-Davidson drops over a concrete levee bank, flies along and lands on the ground. It was a two-storey drop. I saw that and thought, 'Oh my god! That guy has a huge bike, no helmet. How the hell did they pull that off?' But then I saw the 'making of': it was all done on cables. The bike came down on a flying fox. There was no pressure, no skill. The guy just had to be game enough to sit on the bike. In the movie *Ghost Rider*, with Nicolas Cage, there's a scene where he comes off the motorbike and cartwheels down a ramp, Evel Knievel style. All done with cables. They still needed a stunt guy to do it; but my definition of a stunt performer is a little bit different.

Stuntman Hal Needham, whose Hollywood life was 'bone-breaking and death-defying', thought technological advances took all of the reality out of the movies. 'I just can't stand it. Even as a director, I never did that stuff. We did it for real. I can look at it onscreen and go, "That's B.S. That don't work. You can't do that." And so I lose all interest in the film.'

That's another reason why I'm building the Stuntman and Daredevil Hall of Fame, including props and personal memorabilia from friends in the movie business. I want audiences to know that people risked their lives to entertain them at the movies, at the circus, at the live shows. These human beings — exceptionally brave, tough and a little bit crazy — do something out of the ordinary so people feel exhilarated or to make an actor look amazing.

In everything from old westerns to extreme sports, someone

is risking their life to entertain. Everyone has seen a stunt person perform. Every time you turn on the TV or watch a movie you'll see a stunt performer — whether it's someone tripping down a staircase or crashing a car — helping create the illusion.

My goal is to educate people about the movie industry and to give those guys the recognition they deserve.

8
LEAP OF FAITH

In 1996 I decided to build a dirt landing ramp at home and move the take off ramp back and forward to practise the big jumps. I got a better bike and started chasing records and making more of a name for myself.

My new bike was a 1994 Honda CR250. It was only a few years old when I got it and was very superior. It had better suspension and I didn't need to change much on it. I didn't realise it while I was on the older bike but they were like chalk and cheese. That Honda was followed by a few other bikes and eventually a CR500, a bike that was better for the bigger jumps; it had more power and got me to the ramp a lot quicker.

Summernats — the Summer Nationals, an annual car festival held in Canberra — became the launchpad for the next stage of my career.

I like to think that I'm someone who is easy to work with, who doesn't make life hard, who gets the job done. That, at least, is how I got the job with the Summernats in 1996.

The year before they had a guy who was rough around the edges but had attracted some attention. He had persuaded someone to let him have a good car — a genuine Ford GT350 — and said he'd do a jump and the car wouldn't be damaged. He had organised some sponsorship and put a roll cage in the car.

On the day, he set up his jump where the Summernats car show was supposed to be so the show had to be rearranged. He got the cars he was to jump over from Rent A Bomb and put explosives on them. The promoter loaned him a bike to ride around the arena while on fire. The bike was burned to a crisp. When he came to make the jump he miscalculated his speed across the infield and, with fireballs going off around him, came down half way over the cars. It was such a disaster the organisers vowed never to hire another stunt performer. The following year I sold them the idea of jumping twelve trucks on a motorbike. I got the job because of my professional approach.

The truck jumping opportunity came about because I said I would attempt an Australian record: twelve trucks with a 250cc. The records used to be categorised for 125, 250 and 500cc motorbikes. Dale Buggins had jumped eleven trucks before. Since then I have jumped fifteen trucks because the 500cc record was fourteen trucks (and Evel Knievel had jumped fourteen trucks).

One of the sponsors at Summernats was a truck company, who said they could get the trucks if I could do the jump. I knew I could do the distance using the dirt landing ramp but I had to build a landing ramp for Summernats because hiring a scaffolding company would have cost too much. I went to a timber yard where I used to get the timber for the Wall of Fire. I couldn't afford to buy it but asked if I could use it and give it back. I built the frames, but didn't have the plywood to go on the top; that was provided by Summernats. In the end I didn't have enough ply for the ramp to reach the ground. There was a gap of nearly a foot. I thought if I got that far it would be the least of my troubles.

I was excited. It was the first time I had expensive equipment — with matching colour schemes — between my ramps. I was really jumping over the trucks' turntables. If I landed on those I wouldn't have damaged the trucks but I would have messed myself up pretty bad.

I had to put on a mini stunt show beforehand, where I stood on the seat of the bike and rode into the side of a car so I would be catapulted over, with the bike flipping and following me. When I did the stunt the door of the old HQ Holden didn't buckle and the handlebars hit me in the thighs as I flipped over. My legs swelled up instantly. In five minutes I had to jump over twelve trucks. Two girls in my crew, dressed in the colours of the Australian flag, rubbed my legs to relieve the swelling.

When I got on the bike the adrenalin took over and I stopped thinking about the pain in my legs. I did the pass and then the jump. I landed on the ramp but, because we were using the bare minimum of plywood, the back wheel punched a hole into it. The wheel went in, buckled and came out but I held onto the bike and rode to the end. The crowd cheered, people went ballistic and the promoter was over the moon. When we went back to see the huge hole in the ramp we wondered how I survived.

What bothered me most, however, was that after we set up the ramps and went back to the caravan park to clean up before the jump I forgot to bring my white shirt and tie. I had to make that major jump in a blue polo shirt.

The jump made the television news but, as always at Summernats, no-one took a good photograph because it was hard to capture an image of the bike at night.

Night jumping is otherwise preferable because the bikes run better with the night air. Two-stroke motorcycles, relying on a fuel and air mixture, run more crisply in the thinner night air. It's almost like running with the choke on slightly. The downside of jumping at night is cornering with the spotlight in your face as you approach the ramp. Or there may be no lighting at all so you have to use the headlights of your cars for the run-up.

I've been jumping late in the evening at Summernats when the crowd would boo me as I did the run-bys. If it's a big jump you know you only have one chance at it and you have to be in the zone and have your mind right. The jump might be rehearsed but the set up would be moved from somewhere else, so it's like doing it for the first time. Everything else can be exactly the same but something in the back of your mind makes you anxious: Have I done something wrong, have I changed something, have I stuffed this up?

Then you say to yourself: You're here. You said you are going to do this. You've said how much you want to do this. This is what your life's worth. You've got to go. And then you have to be brave enough, prepared to accept the consequences if something bad happens. You made the choice to be there so there's no point later saying I wish I hadn't done that.

People in that situation can also have accidents. For instance, at a fair I could be asked, 'Lawrence, how much time do you need to set up?'

'I need ten minutes.'

'Okay, you've got ten minutes. Go.'

I've had to get all my gear out, get dressed, finish prepping, get on the bike huffing and puffing, and go. Rest time was afterwards.

Stunts at Summernats involved bigger jumps than at regional shows — and we were paid properly — so more professionalism was required. We put the time in to make sure we got it right.

Car stunts were especially complicated. There were so many mechanical things that could go wrong. Safety was important and cars had to be modified, including fuel tanks and roll cages. The crew had to learn how things were planned out, how to get in through the roll cage, and how to get me out. Sometimes I was in so tight I couldn't move to free myself. If I knocked myself out there would be one or two people who knew exactly what to do to get me out in a hurry. Everyone understood we were doing something that involved a big risk but it was a calculated risk.

Is that even possible?

No matter how carefully you plan stunts there's always a chance something will go wrong. One small fun stunt at Summernats involved dropping a car 'left in the wrong area' onto a caravan. Before the crane released the car a streaker ran out and tried to hide under the caravan. After he was safely removed the falling car just caught the edge of its target.

Another stunt involved driving beneath a series of cars on platforms raised on stilts, with the cars dropping as I passed beneath. I envisaged a clear field with a long run-up and six cars. But they put me on an angle with a short run. I requested cars without glass and engines but not only did they give me complete cars, some were also loaded with junk and two had petrol leaking out of them. We could use only four.

In another stunt I drove through cars standing on their ends, with the cars flipping over as I hit them. That time they had done the right thing and stripped the glass and engines out but one car was sitting low at the back. I thought it was because they had removed the shocks. After the stunt one of my team said, 'Oh, Lawrence, you hit them so hard the engine fell out of your car!'

'What?'

'Yeah, the engine's on the ground back there.'

'No, I turned the car off. The engine was still running. There's an engine in this car.'

There was an engine in the boot of one of the car bodies. When it was raised on its end and I hit it, the engine was tossed into the air. There is a golden rule with car stunts: always check for the spare tyre; most cars have them and they are likely to become projectiles. You don't expect an engine to come flying out at you.

Even though we got cars from the wreckers, we spent more time fixing them up and putting roll cages in them than the cars were worth. And they were useless afterwards. I tried to hang onto to them as long as I could. I got three stunts out of one car by rebuilding the front end. Nowadays vehicles are more readily available because people don't keep them as long. When we were younger a Toyota

Corolla would last forever; they could be recycled many times over before they went to the wreckers. It's a lot cheaper now to use better-looking cars.

In the early days I copied other stunts I had seen; not so much lying awake at night imagining something unique, as I did later. I'd see something on TV and think, 'I can do that better.' Someone might have a good idea — jumping over a steam train, for instance — but the rider's gear would be nondescript, the ramps would be unprofessional. I'd think, 'How cool would it be if …'

I wouldn't be thinking I was better or that the jump would be bigger but it would *look* better. That's how I always approached things. As years went on I understood that I had to do something that no-one else had seen. I had to catch the imagination of a promoter. Sometimes I would say, 'What do you think about this?' or even 'Yes, I can do that' and then go away and work out how.

Sometimes I'd just ask, 'Could that be done?' And I'd start reverse engineering. 'No, I reckon I could do that.' Then when people said I couldn't … 'Yeah, you just watch me.'

That's my favourite motivator: the haters or people who say it can't be done — even friends who have known me for years question what I'm doing. When I did the stilt drop, a friend came out and asked, 'Have you tested this? Will it work?'

I said, 'That's what I'm doing tomorrow.'

'We're only a week out!'

'That's all right. I know what I'm doing.'

'Will that hold a car?'

'I'm pretty sure it will. In my mind it will.'

He just shook his head. But he was there when the scaffolding guy I'd known for years erected the stilts and the platforms actually held the cars.

'I told you.'

If I think something is going to work it will work. And if not I will soon fix it so it does work. It's a matter of having the foresight to know what is required to achieve the result and then, if necessary, being adaptable. I think of the worst possible thing that can happen and then start working backwards, to put everything in place that would prevent it. When I do car stunts I look at things like the edge of the bonnet. What if it unhinged and twisted through the windscreen? It could pin me or cut my face or throat. So I use chains and bolts to tie it down. It might never happen. It has never happened during thousands of stunts. But I think, 'What if?'

The stunts themselves can be expensive. The first Tunnel of Fire was done on a shoestring. It cost five hundred dollars just for the hessian and timber, let alone the time. We had to have fire extinguishers recharged. We didn't have sponsors. It wasn't until the bigger jumps later on that I could approach sponsors to cover costs.

Ideas for some of the records were simply about creating something quirky. Setting a record meant someone had to do something first and get it in the media. Then it was there for anyone to challenge it. Once there was a benchmark — an Australian first or a world first — someone could challenge it and perhaps claim a world record.

You have to be diligent with record claims because you will be judged by your peers, other stunt people, and they are ruthless; they will cut you down to size sooner than look at you. If you set about claiming a world record they will be your best researchers because they will find the guy overseas who did the stunt twenty years earlier. I have a pretty good knowledge of the best stunts and records, particularly in Australia, because I love it so much and I know the people and stunt history.

After I'd been doing motorbike jumping for a few years I went to a promoter and asked if they knew about Hans Tholstrup and entrepreneur Dick Smith jumping a double-decker bus over fourteen bikes in 1980. I had found a double-decker bus and reckoned if I got it for the right price I could set a new record. His eyes lit up and within a week I had a double-decker bus.

At Summernats in January 2003 I broke the old world record by jumping over eighteen motorbikes in a double-decker bus. Twenty-two bikes were lined up but I landed on some. I had been working on the stunt for nearly a year. I was ecstatic. The next year I jumped a double-decker over thirty-eight motorcycles. The following year I extended it to forty-five.

Crowd pleaser

My death-defying stunt at Summernats in January 2006 was to replicate the spiral jump from the 1974 James Bond movie *The Man with the Golden Gun*, when Roger Moore even mentioned Evel Knievel. In the film an AMC Hornet X jumps off one ramp, performs a complete three hundred and sixty degree barrel roll as it crosses a river, lands on another ramp and drives off undamaged. I was hoping I'd do the same and drive the car back on the trailer instead of picking it up with a crane.

It wasn't to be.

We did the research and had the car set up so that the steering column was in the middle and the balance was even. The spiral was good but the car didn't twist as quickly as it should have. It hit the ramp and ended up on cardboard boxes covered in a tarp.

It was still a good, spectacular stunt and even though it failed I think it was a crowd pleaser.

Just before my stunt there was a display of cars drifting around the track. One of them lost control, went through the fence and hit some children. During the pandemonium that followed I was sent out to do some two-wheeling to keep the crowd entertained. I felt bad performing while someone was hurt at the other end and I was sure the spiral stunt would be cancelled. The ambulances arrived

First double-decker bus jump over 20 motorcycles: the Irish Evel Knievel.

Jumping over 15 semitrailers at Summernats (1999).

My second most favourite thing to do on two wheels.

Double-decker buses are also great for jumping over (2002).

but I didn't know how serious the injuries were. Even though I had convinced myself our performance wouldn't go ahead I was told to start the jump.

'Really?'

'We're going to have more of a problem if you don't go.'

So I strapped myself in, did a few run-bys, performed the stunt and crashed. I wasn't hurt but the ambulance driver insisted I go around to the medical centre to be checked out. When I emerged from the medical centre I was surrounded by reporters wanting to talk to me. But a guy was there with one of the children who had been hurt. I was embarrassed because they wanted to interview me about the stunt while that poor guy was there worried about his child. I said, 'No, we're not filming here. We need to go back to the arena.'

In the paper the next day I had no coverage but a story said, 'Stunt driver crashes into crowd'. The only stunt driver there that day was me. I was angry. And then the organisers had the hide to complain that I charged them for a stunt that didn't work. I suspect people would have been less impressed if the jump had succeeded. The crash was more spectacular. I just showed them it was hard.

Summernats was a lot of work for the whole crew — fifteen to twenty people depending on the stunts. While we were booked together in a motel, most of our time was spent at the venue. We turned up on the Saturday, set up, remained there most of the day and night and packed up when everyone started to leave.

We were in the centre of the arena and didn't go out with the public. The infield had cars on show until four o'clock. Then we had four hours to build a Tunnel of Fire or build a ramp, set vehicles out and make sure everything was right. It was a huge job that put a lot of stress on my friends and family. Everyone was running around like maniacs.

We employed people for certain things and friends and family did what they could. If we had to build a Tunnel of Fire, everyone had to lug stuff and throw hessian over. Dad was like my number one crew chief. You can see him in the background in most of the videos of my stunts.

Many of the ramps at Summernats were hard to set up, especially for the big jumps. It was torture putting up the plywood for the down ramps. It was in the middle of summer. People were loading plywood, sliding the sheets, screwing all the individual sheets down. Crews of a dozen people were screwing plywood. We would go up to Canberra the week before to start setting up half the ramp; then on the night we'd screw the timber down.

I was supervising as well as having safety meetings with people running the show. I had to throw on my gear and get ready to go. It was a huge task and very stressful — an absolute nightmare. It was such a relief to hop in the seat of the car or on the motorbike. I don't like that feeling, the absolute bedlam. It's the bit I hate the most about stunt work. With so much rushing, when you're trying to keep to a deadline, mistakes can be made.

I would get so focused I became very short with the crew. They knew when to stay away. I wasn't nervous; I planned everything to the letter. Nothing could go wrong apart from the things I couldn't control. But the pressure I put on myself — for everything to work so the crowd would be entertained; for everything to be okay for my family and friends, who were scared for my safety — made me abrupt and angry.

Before the big jumps at Summernats I'd go round to my team, to friends and relatives, and shake their hands and give them a hug or a kiss. I'd say, 'I apologise for how I've been today.' They'd say, 'It's okay, we know you now.'

For the first couple of years it was pretty horrible for them. I'd tell them, 'It's just the pressure of getting it right. This is my time to thank you. If anything happens to me I don't want you to forever hold a grudge against me for being a bit cranky.' They knew I wasn't angry with them; it was just my way of dealing with it.

But they warned new people to beware of me on the day.

When I got on the bike or in the car I heaved a huge sigh of relief. 'Now I can do the stunt.' And afterwards, when I landed the jump, all the pressure was released because the biggest thing to do then was pack up. In some ways pack up is the best part because you can just stop and reflect. There's no pressure. Everyone just gets on and does their job.

Despite my temper, most of the crew kept coming back. They say they enjoyed it. It was a great opportunity, especially if they were interested in cars; they could help me and see all the things that Summernats had to offer.

My cousin Simone was with me for nine years of Summernats — plus when I jumped my house, when I jumped 'Monte Cristo', at regionals shows, and the Easter Show. She has known me all her life and came to my twenty-first birthday party when her brothers played barmen. They would come down for family holidays at 'Monte Cristo'; all the family in the car for seven hours from Tumbi Umbi on the Central Coast of New South Wales.

Simone heard about me when she was young: cousin Lawrence who was a bit crazy and did silly things with cars and bikes. But when I started doing Summernats she was involved straight away, making posters and books and going to the shows. She was in charge of dressing me, handing me the gloves and boots and everything in order to get me ready.

She says she was afraid for me all the time but trusted that I wouldn't do it if I thought something was going to go wrong. Otherwise, if I was silly enough to do it ...

Simone had a couple of friends who came to help at Summernats. One was a mechanic who brought his father along. They were both mechanics and were tremendous supporters. They also thought I was crazy but were the first to put their hands up to help if it was needed.

Charlie Ford, my friend from schooldays, is an electrician who made a few things for the stunts, including a pyrotechnics box to set off the fireworks. He is very aware of the potential for something to go wrong. We did our research but a lot of luck came with it. Charlie reckons most of the crowds came to see me come off. 'They don't come to see you succeed. They come to see carnage. That's part of the thrill.'

Charlie's wife Sharon also was involved in the set up. She folded a lot of boxes. When I crashed, that's where I'd land. Behind the scenes Sharon helped cleaning up and making sure people didn't get in the way. She says she was always afraid for me, especially while I was getting ready, but the atmosphere at Summernats, with everyone cheering, somehow took the fear away. 'Once it was all over it was worth it.' She thought being part of the entertainment at Summernats was a good weekend — while we were in the centre, not among the drunks, fighting the crowd.

There's a difference between doing shows for families and kids and doing shows for drunken yobbos or petrol heads. I maintain that if I can entertain that crowd I can't be bad because they are one of the hardest. In America they'll cheer two snails racing up a wall. Here they throw beers at you and tell you how they can do a better job.

Wanna beer?

Jumping twelve trucks was my biggest jump to date and I did more run-bys than usual. People in the grandstand were yelling out, 'Just do it! Stop fucking around. Just do the jump.' If I'd done another run-by they would have strung me up. With fifty thousand intoxicated people looking on I always felt there was less risk doing a dangerous stunt than in pulling out.

When we finished a show there was usually a band or strippers on the other side of the arena. So the crowd would rush across to get the best possible position to see the naked girls (in thirteen years at Summernats I saw just two pairs of boobs because I was working in the middle). It was like a wave. Whoosh. Everyone in our crew had to be assigned to stand beside a vehicle or piece of equipment to make sure it wasn't broken or stolen.

People would take the keys out of the stunt cars so we couldn't move them. Once when we were taking ramps apart a bloke stood next to us urinating before heading over to listen to the next act. Others would come over and shake our hands and tell us we were awesome. But they were extremely drunk. We were just happy to be heading out of there.

Sometimes when I had to leave landing ramps overnight I'd come back in the morning to find them pushed over or to discover a car pushed to the top and hanging over the edge.

I'm the total opposite of the Summernats crowd. I don't drink. I don't smoke. I don't go to nightclubs. I don't think it's cool to call out for women to expose their breasts.

During the day Summernats was all right but after four o'clock on Saturday night things grew more tense. Originally they did a super cruise down Canberra's Northbourne Avenue. When that was stopped they cruised around the oval at Summernats. Then to fill in time there would be a huge fireworks display. I provided the additional entertainment. But because the oval was so big I had to perform the stunts in different locations so everyone could see them: two Walls of Fire, two Tunnels of Fire, two motorbike jumps. It was a big job. I don't think they appreciated how much work was involved. Though they did appreciate that I got in and out on schedule, did what I said I was going to do and didn't create any hassles for the organisers. That's why they kept inviting me back.

Every so often they would complain if a stunt didn't work.

'You didn't land the car on the other ramp.'

'Well I hit the ramp. I just didn't land too well.'

They didn't understand there was more to it than just doing the jump.

Summernats received a lot of bad press, focusing on the bad elements Summernats attracted. It would have been a nightmare to run. But they treated me well, especially in the early years, and the money was fair reward for the work we put in.

It certainly wasn't all bad. There is footage of my first time at Summernats when I drove around the track waving to the crowd. They threw full beer cans at me.

Later they would bring the beer to me.

'Wanna beer, mate? Wanna beer?'

Whatever I did the crowds seem to love it. There were always people coming up afterwards saying, 'What you did was amazing!' They liked to see someone risking his life for their entertainment.

It's funny how other people perceive danger. My friend Charlie thought the stunt where I drove a Rolls Royce through a bus was the scariest. He was taking photos that night. The bus was gutted and a ramp ran up to the end. I had to drive the Rolls Royce through the bus and then through the front. There were false panels at either end so the car didn't stop dead. But I got to the end and the fireworks went off and I stopped dead. The car went up in flames. I was strapped in. Charlie says his heart stopped then. He thought I was gone. But I got out.

Another guy trying to drive through four buses got decapitated. I wasn't worried about the fire. Fire is unpredictable but it is controllable and you can take precautions. It probably won't be the fire that kills you; it will be smoke or lack of oxygen. The race suits are designed to keep fire at bay.

Michael, my nephew, thinks the bikes are impressive but that there is more risk involved in car stunts. You are in the car, crashing into other cars, there is all that metal, you could get trapped and there is all that potential for fire. With a bike, he says, you can fall off and separate from any related danger.

The car is like a big cocoon and you are strapped in your seat. You're a peanut in a tin can they have thrown down a hill. If you don't mind getting bumped around a bit, having bruises a week later from the harness, it's all right. You will just feel sore and sorry afterwards. Whereas with a motorbike jump, if you land hard, you feel like your kidneys are still up in your mouth a week later. And there's not much to protect you if it doesn't go well.

Of course, things can still go wrong in a car. You rely on the roll cage and the harness. If one of those fails it will be worse than a bike stunt because you will be jammed into something protruding into the car.

Sharon has had the pleasure of being on the bonnet of a car that I drove through a Wall of Fire. She thought that was scary. Yet the Wall of Fire is one of the lamest things I do. There's a bit of science to it: you're not there long enough to get burnt; all that's burning is the wood you go through. People still think it's awesome.

Sharon has known me since she was sixteen and has been involved in many tricks and stunts. Her first stunt also involved a car bonnet — one with sheet metal bent up the sides and a car seat attached. We dragged her around the paddock behind a car. 'It will be all right Sharon. Get on. Have a ride. We won't drive fast.' It was muddy. It was wet. It was cold. I'm sure she had fun.

Simone thinks the Tunnel of Fire at the Summernats was the scariest because it was longer. It was fun for the crew because everyone was involved. Everyone had a part in building the tunnel. It freaked her out, though, because she imagined the fire taking away the oxygen. She had horrible visions of me not making it through. But she says it was the most memorable stunt. It looked good. It was spectacular.

Jumping a double-decker bus over a row of motorbikes was one of my more embarrassing stunts. It was a quirky thing rather than dangerous. But afterwards people said, 'That was awesome, that was the best thing I've ever seen. You're crazy, man, you're crazy. You're a bloody legend.' Yet, when I jumped a bike over fifteen trucks, guys came up to my saying, 'I could have done that' and 'Jake could have done that. He rides motorbikes. He could have done that.'

Perceptions about what is going to kill me are totally out of whack.

When I see stunts that have gone wrong, I analyse why.

The Tunnel of Fire is a good example. People have been killed attempting to break that record. Stunt performers were making long tunnels with chicken wire down the side. That was great for holding the straw but if they shot out the side they could be entangled in the wire and burn to death. Or if it wasn't designed properly the tunnel roof would collapse on them.

So I designed mine with timber down the side as a skeleton to hold the hessian with wire going out like guy ropes on a tent. If I came out through the wall I wouldn't be strung up on the wire and burn.

My first tunnel was unassisted, with no fire gear other than a fireproof balaclava and dousing myself with water. The problem with dousing yourself with water and riding into a very hot Tunnel of Fire is that the water turns to steam and you still get burnt.

The tunnels for Summernats weren't for records, apart from a tandem ride (I put my wife on the back and told people that's how I stopped my back from getting burnt). They were still painful to do because building the tunnels was very time consuming and I needed lots of friends and family to help. I didn't know if they were going to light properly, I was relying on people pouring the fuel, and I was relying on people to light it without getting burnt. Tunnels were dangerous for the crew. People say getting burned alive is one of the most horrible ways to die.

You wouldn't wish that on your worst enemies.

9

ALL THE FUN OF THE FAIR

Showgrounds weren't suitable for setting records but they were my bread and butter.

After the 1996 record trucks jump I rested on my laurels and wasn't thinking about more records, just concentrating on getting more fair shows: I'd take my bikes, ramp trailer and gear and jump over three cars lengthways, do a wall of fire, some wheelies, and a jump where I chased a car and jumped over the top of it.

That was how I earned a living.

The Summernats crowd wouldn't appreciate some of the stunts I did at the shows. Whatever the difficulty of distance or timing they would think, 'Big deal.' But the show crowds, who weren't drunk and were a bit more engaged, would say, 'Oh man, if he hadn't timed that just right he'd have been killed. How would you do that!' People clapped when I drove on. They climbed through fences to congratulate me and say hello. They appreciated what we were doing.

It is a terrific feeling when you do a show and everything comes off according to plan. No-one is hurt and everyone is happy.

The paddock at 'Monte Cristo' was important because it provided the opportunity to test and develop ideas for stunts. We'd make sure the stunts were right. And we had fun. A lot of people were involved in the preparation. I wouldn't have been able to bring an idea to fruition unless they were there to share it with me.

My nephew Michael was a long-time member of the team. He learned to ride motorbikes on his father's farm, 'Ivanhoe', at Junee Reefs. Everyone rode bikes on the farms. That's what we did on the weekends. I would take my bikes out and ride with Michael. I'd show him how to jump dam banks; picking a spot, shaping it with a shovel and helping him measure his speed.

When his family moved into town they had no space to ride so Michael left his bike at 'Monte Cristo' and rode there whenever he wanted. When he came over we'd get his bike out and do wheelies up and down the hill.

'They were things I thought was normal,' he says now. 'That's what your uncle does with you. But when you get a bit older you realise not everyone does that sort of thing.'

Michael rode with me in the paddocks for fun and when I rehearsed for shows. We did lots of jumps, just using what we had to begin with: an old car or an old motorbike. I would put on some pads and practise crashes by running into cardboard boxes on the back of a car. It was just mates having fun; nothing for a show. I'd get an idea and we'd muster up whatever we needed to make it happen.

By the time he was twelve, Michael was jumping four or five cars in the back paddock. He was only going over the bonnets but I'd set the ramps up for him, he'd make a jump and we'd pull the ramp back and put more cars in.

That was just how we spent our time. He'd watch me make a jump, then I'd ask if he wanted a go, getting him to jump something bigger. Everything was a stepping stone. I'd motivate him through affirmation, letting him know he could do it. 'I'll stand beside the ramp and give you the speed and you can go for it.'

Now that he has his own kids, Michael realises how brave he was then. I had to answer to his mother, who saw me break my ankle and feared the same thing could happen to Michael. But I never let him attempt something I wasn't confident about. And Michael doesn't seem to regret it: 'I want my kids to experience those good times. The mateship. Going for a ride. You can't explain how good it is to go for a ride with your mates. You can have anything playing on your mind but when you get out on your bike that is the last thing you are worrying about. All you are thinking about is riding your bike.'

Michael also understood my dream to follow in the footsteps of the old-school stuntmen. It wasn't about having the best bikes or the best gear; it was just about being a stuntman.

Initially he wasn't part of the shows but when he started motorbike racing and developed more bike skills he joined in the stunts. The first major show he did with me was at Wagga Wagga Cricket Ground. He was a young kid doing low-key jumps like the ring of fire but he helped develop a younger fan base. He did a few single car jumps and people jumps and moved onto bigger jumps as he grew.

Michael always helped with the set up, running around in his gear before going behind the trailer to put his jacket and helmet on. He'd hop on his bike and do a jump, then take his gear off and help set up more stunts.

He travelled with me to Sydney, Summernats, Perth and a lot of the small shows. Perth was Michael's favourite. He was fourteen and it was a big show. He did the Ring of Fire and jumped some people from the audience.

On the money

The earlier shows were only a glimpse of what we were doing in the paddock — some of the better things but only a glimpse. I would do much harder stunts at home, where it didn't matter if I fell off. An act for a show had to be as safe as it could be, a controlled performance. If I had to do more than one stunt I couldn't do the biggest stunt first. I couldn't risk hurting myself because I had to continue with the rest of the show.

With the big jumps there was even a risk if wanted to practise beforehand. Did I want to keep tempting fate? Should I practise two weeks before the show when there was a chance of falling off and then not being able to do the show? I had promised that I would be there to do the jump and it was in all the catalogues and flyers and TV promotion.

Occasionally at a show I did a jump a second time because I wasn't satisfied with the first one. That's usually not the preference because it detracts from the show if you do it twice. If a jump is supposed to be hard it's best to do it once, even if it's a bit sketchy.

Unlike Summernats, the window for set up at agricultural shows was very brief. There was a lot of pressure. It was not just getting there and riding a motorbike and having fun. The small shows usually involved a day trip. We got there, unpacked quickly, set up, waited around for hours and did the show before the mad rush to pack up and get home. We were always pulling things apart and putting them together, using basic tools with limited access to power. Once we'd undone bolts half a dozen times the threads would be stripped. Sometimes something would break or we'd misplace a tool and struggle to take a ramp down.

There wasn't time to do a few little jumps to warm up. I had to do it on the money straight away in front of a crowd. It put pressure on everyone around. And there were a lot of people from the show societies trying to micromanage every little thing. I could be doing a moving car jump and someone would walk out across the track. No matter how organised the crew was I had to be continually on the lookout for something like that. Every show presented a new list of challenges: cables, pegs, horses, fireworks.

But that was our lifestyle for many years. Every weekend or every second weekend Dad would load up the station wagon and away we'd go.

I've been to hundreds of showgrounds across Australia, from Broken Hill to Darwin, Perth and Rockhampton. I've kept all the programs and itinerary lists. The only major shows I didn't do as a motorbike rider by myself were the Royal Melbourne Show and the Royal Adelaide Show. When we went to Brewarrina — east of Bourke in north-western New South Wales, with a population of two thousand Aboriginal people — we got the best reception and sold more souvenirs than we did at any of the Royal Shows.

Once we did a road trip, three shows in three days. And we did some car stunts at a big bikie show in Blacktown, Sydney. Simone was scared. She wasn't sure it would be what they wanted. But they liked it. Most people who are interested in cars or bikes like to see them put through their paces or put to a test.

I have been least welcome in the local region. I did the Junee Show for free in October 1989 — the largest crowd they ever had — and I haven't been asked back since, perhaps because I'm just the local boy and I'm not worth paying for. I have never done a motorcycle show at Wagga Wagga Show. Before I got the booking for a two-wheel driving show there I had to do an audition. At the Royal Easter Show the following year, when I was driving in the Toyota team, I saw the president of the Wagga Wagga Show, who was suddenly impressed by my two-wheel act.

Just before I moved up to Queensland in 1993 I had a stunt show on the Junee property. The Junee Show was on at the same time and from the showground you could see our property and the set up for my motorbike stunts. A guy who ran a fairy floss van at the show asked if he could set up on our site while the stunts were on. I said that was fine; the more the merrier. He was impressed by what he saw and said he had asked people at the show society what was going on. They told him it was an idiot pretending to be a stunt man. He reckoned he made more money at my event than he did at the show.

You never get recognition in your home town.

The Canberra showground is one of my favourites. It is the best to perform at because it's one of the biggest. There's plenty of room to run-up and plenty of stopping area. And it's nice and flat. It's also where I did a lot of my world record jumps and had some of the largest crowds.

Other than that you are dealing with uneven surfaces, cow manure, horse manure, horse jumps, people, dogs and trailers. Sometimes I had to weave between obstacles in the run up to the ramp because otherwise there was no room to do the stunt. The worst places were rodeo rings, with churned-up, soft ground. It was like bouncing across the surface of Mars. No, Mars is probably smoother.

I injured my knee two weeks before a city show due to a bad run-up. I over-accelerated on the jump, landed on the back wheel, jerked a handlebar from my hand, lost it and washed out. The bike span around and the handlebar struck my kneecap. It hurt like all hell and I couldn't walk properly for a couple of weeks.

Giving back

Three weeks before I did the Tunnel of Fire at 'Monte Cristo' in 1997 we attempted one at a charity fair. We were a bit rushed and hadn't rehearsed the pouring of fuel. When we were ready to go, my Dad was on one side and a friend of his was on the other side to start it burning. Other lighters were afraid to get close and threw their sticks, missing the sides or landing them on the roof where there was no fuel. When the first part of the tunnel was alight I took off but when I reached the second part of the tunnel it hadn't caught fire. We couldn't put it out and start again. Half the tunnel burned to the ground. It was embarrassing at the time but made for a better story when I attempted it again. I had to spend more money for timber and hessian but I was determined to set the record. The next time we rehearsed and did test burnings. We learned a lot from it but still weren't prepared for how much fire there was going to be.

Publicity shot (1996).

Performing at one of the many agricultural shows across Australia.

Human catapult stunt for a charity event. The car is set on fire this time.

The wall of fire is one of the most popular stunts I do at shows.

We did a lot of charity shows. Mum and Dad set the example, raising money for different causes. The annual 'Monte Cristo' Ball, in its forty-second year in 2014, was charity oriented. We always had a sense we should give back, money or time. My eldest sister had a daughter with MPS (Mucopolysaccharidoses), a rare genetic disorder. She only lived to five years of age but there was a lot of fundraising when she was alive.

I was always happy to help out charities but they didn't always make it easy for me. People didn't appreciate the costs involved. They would call asking if I could do a charity event but they couldn't afford to pay me. But then they wouldn't put me on the sponsors' list or give me any credit. In addition to risking my life it cost me money to be there to perform. I had to drive there, bring all the gear, plus my time. They would otherwise treat me well but what they classified as free was not free.

I once was asked to do a charity event at Cessnock for a percentage of the gate. I wasn't keen but said I'd do it if they also paid for fuel costs. A few thousand people saw the show but afterwards I was given only two hundred dollars — what came in between seven thirty and eight thirty when I was scheduled to perform. It was as if people who were coming to watch me would only turn up at seven thirty.

It's hard dealing with promoters like that. Often you find if you charge big money you are treated properly; if you do people favours or charge token amounts you get treated like rubbish. If you are desperate for work you'll take anything and get treated poorly; if you don't need the work people throw heaps of money at you and treat you like royalty.

I don't plan to perform at shows anymore. Show societies, though they have improved in recent years, had committees of people who had been on the farm for decades, and were only used to dealing with sheep and cows. Once a year they would come to town and attempt to be professional event organisers. In earlier times it was simpler and they could get away with it. As more emphasis was placed on marketing, sponsorship and finance they were out of their depth.

Now the rides and entertainment are run by companies. Not so long ago the people who brought the show rides were families, living out of rundown caravans. Stunt performers were treated like showies. I didn't like the stigma attached to that. Even if they were paying me thousands of dollars I wasn't as important as the horses or the dog trials. I was just the stupid guy on the motorbike. And they would make me wait. If they put me behind schedule and the crowd was angry — because they hadn't come to see the horse jumping — that would reflect on me.

Sometimes I was even put on after the fireworks. You can be the best show in the world but after the fireworks have gone off people start leaving. I could be doing wheel stands down the main straight while people were walking out. And the organiser would have the hide to tell me, 'Your show sucked, Lawrence. People didn't stay to see you ride.'

When the show business became less successful and they couldn't sustain the events over more than one day they would blame the entertainers that cost more, like the stunt drivers: 'We could afford two pig racers for what we paid for you!'

Cost was the main reason so many jumps have been attempted at 'Monte Cristo'.

While Summernats and showgrounds provided an income, 'Monte Cristo' only cost me time and set up and I could control it more. I had to have insurance to go somewhere and I had to take all the equipment, which meant having trailers and transport vehicles. I decided I'd rather control the stunts, set them up myself, and make sure everything was right, or else regroup, without being dictated by a showground's timeframe.

The dirt landing ramp at 'Monte Cristo' also came in handy for car stunts; even stunts designed to fail. One of those involved creating a spectacular crash by jumping a double-decker bus and landing on a row of cars. I speared a 1980 XD Ford Falcon into the roof of an unfortunate catch car. I would have preferred to have been going a little faster and cartwheeled over a few cars. It always looks better if you park the car upside down.

It was exciting chasing records, doing the big jumps. I wanted to get as many records as I could. But it was also a struggle. Sometimes I see that people have jumped further and I think I would have done more if I had the backing and the resources. No-one was offering money for me to make big jumps.

But it was never really about the money. I got a kick out of doing it and the crew got a kick out of being a part of it. Money helped because it cost money but even if I couldn't have made a living from it I would have been doing it anyway. I would go out and do the stunts in the back paddock if no-one was watching.

It's me I'm doing it for. It's great to make money and it's great to get recognition but my trophies are the photographs on my wall. That's what I look at each morning. And even then I sometimes think, 'I could do that better.'

10
THE LEGEND CONTINUES

I remember as a kid going past the Tourist Information Centre in Tarcutta Street, Wagga Wagga. It had land on either side and I thought it would be a good building to jump over. Years went by and I realised the huge gasworks on an adjacent block would be in the way of the run-up or landing. But when the gasworks was torn down there was lots of extra space. I thought, 'This will be good!'

In 1999 I went to the Mayor of Wagga Wagga and told him I wanted to jump the Tourist Information Centre in November and that I'd do it for charity. He thought it was a good idea and it would be good publicity for the city.

While I was waiting to see the Mayor someone else was there with me: a reporter from the local paper, the *Daily Advertiser*. He asked who I was and why I wanted to see the Mayor. The next day it was in the paper.

That ruffled a few feathers.

The council agreed to talk to me about it but the guy responsible for tourism didn't take kindly to my plans. They would have had to shut down the information centre during the jump and he wanted no part of it. He said they could find another building for me to jump over.

It got close to the time I wanted to do the jump but the council hadn't given the go ahead. So I let the paper know the jump might not be happening after all and they put a picture of me on the front page, standing at the entrance of 'Monte Cristo'. The story — The City of Good Sports is no good sport — said I might have to jump over that building because Wagga Wagga Council had refused to let me jump the information centre.

That didn't go down well either.

We had another meeting that wasn't quite as pleasant. 'What do we need to do to get this done?' In other words, 'Do it and go away.'

When I next spoke to the tourism manager, I observed, 'Where there's a will there's a way.' His response: 'I have better things to do than waste my time with some idiot who wants to jump over a bloody building.' People later told me they didn't even know where the Tourist Information Centre was until I jumped over it.

We set it all up and it became a big event. People were everywhere. They had to close down a road. It was a charity event but we didn't have enough people collecting; we could have done so much better. It was a big jump. I couldn't see where I was landing but made it over.

It was one of many occasions where someone congratulating me shook my hand and wouldn't let go. People go to watch live jumps because they are unusual; there is a real element of risk. They get drawn into it because they invest their time and emotion in the person doing the stunt. It has an overwhelming effect on some people. And I believe there are people who will long remember seeing Lawrence Legend jumping over something.

The Wagga Wagga Tourist Information Centre is part of my tally of the five jumped buildings (now including my own house, 'Monte Cristo', the King's Own Hotel at The Rock, thirty two kilometres south-west of Wagga Wagga, and a cottage at 'Monte Cristo').

Jumping that building also made a physical link between my stunt career and tourism in the region — though it is something that doesn't seem to be welcomed in all quarters. I talk about Junee all the time. You can't speak about my work without mentioning the word 'Junee', the small country town that I come from. Another fantastic ambassador for Junee is rugby league player and coach Laurie Daley.

In the same month a Canadian TV company came over to film a couple of stunts and asked me what I wanted to do. I chose a jump over an aeroplane and a blindfold jump (even though I hadn't yet thought how I would do either).

Johnny Fogwell had the world record for jumping ten cars blindfolded. He was assisted by a walkie-talkie system, guiding him up to the ramp. I wondered if I could beat that.

Part of my riding show was to wheel-stand the length of a field with a blindfold over my head. It wasn't too hard if you knew how to ride in a straight line. So I did a test run with a part blindfold, where I could just see the difference between sky and land and make out silhouettes. Then I discovered that where I did practise jumps at home there was a mark in the road left by water erosion. If I rode too close as I approached a jump it would draw me in. I figured I could put it to good use if I rode blindfolded: I could plan the jump as usual by calculating how far back to run if I needed to jump a certain distance and the cut in the road could guide me to the ramp.

The TV company came to 'Monte Cristo' for the blindfold jump, later to be broadcast on the series *Life and Dare: The Science of Daredevils*. I used two blindfolds: the practice blindfold and a proper one over the top. They put a camera in my helmet so people could see I really was blind. I took off to do the jump and counted down so I knew when to crouch as I hit the ramp. I was riding the more powerful CR500 that I had used on other jumps but the bike started bucking and I lost my nerve. It was a stinking hot day, I was wearing leathers and the bike was getting hot. I pulled the blindfolds away and returned to the start. My nephew Michael put the blindfolds back in place, tapped my arm and said, 'You're right.'

I took off. This time the bike followed the groove all the way down, leaped off the jump and landed on the other side. Once it was in the air I could feel the trajectory was right. I was extremely happy. It could have been so nasty. My take-off ramp was only three feet wide. I could easily have crashed into the side and made a big mess of it.

Guinness World Records wanted me to do it again for them, taping over my eyes. But I wasn't interested. I had broken Johnny's record and that was enough for me.

Up in the air

We filmed the aeroplane jump at a property at Coolamon, sixty kilometres away from Junee. I had considered the stunt before because a friend of Dad's had an ultra-light that resembled a hang glider. We did some test jumps but it didn't look much like a plane and I wasn't enthusiastic.

I was talking about it with an ultra-light pilot during a 'Monte Cristo' Ball. He said he would like to help but his plane wasn't registered and he didn't want to be identified. The farmer who owned the fields where he flew let us perform the stunt and we mowed a strip with a cross intersection, where we built the jumps about sixteen feet off the ground.

The pilot had practised, I knew the jumps and within a week the TV company from Canada came out to film. It was a hot summer's day and the wind was blowing a gale, with turbulences blasting across the flats. The pilot still did brilliantly. I watched him come down, darting about in the breeze, and just before the ramp he would get the plane perfectly level and fly straight through, sometimes three feet off the ground, sometimes with the wheels clipping the grass. I thought, 'He's got this nailed. I have no problems here.'

However there was a problem with the ramps, which still had the sponsors' banners from the jump over the Tourist Information Centre. The wind caught the banners and dragged the ramps off their marks. That was more than disconcerting if I was in the middle of a run. We removed the banners and reset the ramps. On my first practice jump the wind caught me and took me offline, two feet away from the edge of a twelve-foot landing ramp. 'This isn't good.'

We did some more timing runs and a few more jumps to coordinate the bike with the plane but the wind made it too dangerous. We were likely to make a mistake and someone was going to be killed. I didn't care if the TV cameras were there or not. I said we should come back the next day at daybreak when the wind was down.

I was there at dawn the next day but the film crew was half an hour late. They stopped for breakfast and the wind had picked up. The flags on the ramps were flying as if they were rigid. We got on with it quickly. On the first jump the plane was too early but I made the jump safely. On the second jump I was too early. The third jump was spot on so I asked for one more and they got the shots they needed.

Apart from the wind I didn't think it was dangerous. The pilot and I were confident in our respective abilities. He thought I was more at risk because I had further to fall. Michael thought it was my most memorable jump. He said he could see the big gap I had to cross ramp-to-ramp and could tell if the aeroplane wasn't flying low enough.

Two other stuntmen had done a similar jump, but over a Pitts Special, an aerobatic plane with a wingspan of twenty feet (just over six metres). The plane I jumped had a thirty-foot wingspan, a world record at the time. The Guinness Book of Records now recognises the distance between the bike and the plane, rather than the wingspan jumped.

The documentary the Canadians produced is quite interesting, not the least for the way it shows how the North Americans dramatise everything. If I had more time and a better budget to set it up it could have looked more spectacular. But that's what used to kill me, figuratively: time and money. I either had one or the other or neither.

There is always risk involved when something has to be done there

In my prime. Studio photo shoot (1996).

Wheel stands. Everyone loves a good wheelie.

Getting ready for my return jump at Bolton Park where I crashed in 1991. This time it's 20 cars in 2000.

Flying high. I was so happy to make this jump in front of a crowd of 10,000 strong. That's my Dad watching on. He always believed in me.

and then. That's probably why I rarely had second thoughts about a jump: I never had time to change my mind.

I was fortunate then because the pilot was very talented. If I do the stunt again it will be on a Harley and I'll have to find another pilot. The problem now will be that the Civil Aviation Safety Authority requires the plane to be six metres clear of the ground — so my ramps will have to be huge.

In the year 2000 I returned to the venue of my 1991 accident. The Gumi festival had ceased but there was talk of a Guinness Book of World Records attempt to create the world's largest bowl of fried rice. They needed another event to support it.

Someone suggested that I could be involved and I immediately thought of going back to Bolton Park to try the jump again. There would be five more cars but with a much more modern, conventional bike than the old CB360 twin. I was confident with twenty cars — that was one more than Evel Knievel had jumped.

I started going to the meetings to organise it. I had done the original jump for nothing but this time I needed to cover costs: around four thousand dollars to cover insurance and to carry the equipment around. It got a lot of publicity and plans progressed well but I had to sit through countless meetings about how to cook a ton of fried rice.

The gentleman I knew from the Ford dealership in Wagga Wagga was still there from the time I had the accident. I asked if they could again provide the cars to jump over. He went to his boss, who refused, citing the damage I'd done to two of their cars previously. But he convinced his boss, saying I'd improved since then and had really good ramps. They supplied virtually new cars, fleet cars, all the same model with low mileage. The cars for the first jump were a mish-mash of used cars.

I couldn't replicate the original jump because they had changed the layout of the venue. I had to run the jump on the opposite axis. It was a big jump but the modern CR250 was a lot more powerful and got to speed quickly so I was pretty confident. I set the ramps up and everything was looking polished and professional. I had the same commentator, the local TV news anchor, and the radio station was doing a live cross. Admission was free and the crowd was around ten thousand strong, twice the size as at the original jump.

After the fried rice cook-off everyone was waiting for the jump. I did half a dozen run-bys but it still wasn't a textbook jump. I had too much power when I left the ramp and the front wheel stayed up in the air so I landed back wheel heavy. I managed to hang on but only just pulled up on the grass, short of the roadway and people standing beyond. I dropped the bike, performed a bit of a roll and stood up to the applause of the crowd. I was ecstatic.

I left the bike there and walked back to the ramp. People were spilling into the arena. They were overwhelmed.

The jump ended up being bigger than Dale Buggins' jump over twenty-five cars, ten feet longer than his farthest; although mine was twenty cars, the cars were bigger and my trajectory was higher.

The gloves I wore were auctioned off and raised six hundred dollars for charity. I signed autographs and met some fans. One guy came up and shook my hand and wouldn't let go. He was an older man and kept saying it was the most amazing thing he'd ever seen and he didn't know what to do afterwards. He was supposed to go home and mow his lawns but it seemed insignificant to go home and do such a mundane thing when I'd just risked my life to thrill people.

I had an overwhelming sense of achievement. Even though it was ten years later, it was like a rubber stamp: 'Done.' I knew I could do it! What's next?

It certainly wasn't the end of my record breaking period. Soon to come was the jump over 'Monte Cristo'.

11
A Promise is Kept

A friend of the family said that when I was young, wandering around 'Monte Cristo', I told him I was going to jump a bike over the house. I don't remember the conversation but Dad always told the story and I came to believe doing the jump was a possibility.

In 2001 I was approached by an American TV company that was making a show called *Stuntman's World Tour* and looking for stunt people from around the world to film performing exclusive stunts. They asked if I had anything special coming up. I said, 'I've got something a bit special. How about if I jump over Australia's most haunted house?'

I could hear the cogs turning from the other side of the planet.

'Really? What do you mean?'

'It will be the largest free-standing building to be jumped over but it will also be the most haunted.'

'Does this house exist? Who owns it? Would you be able to get permission?'

'I'm pretty sure I'll be able to but I'll double check.'

So I went to Dad, 'Look, this is what we want to do …'

'Yeah, yeah, not a problem. You're not going to hurt the roof. You'll just bounce off it if you hit it.'

I might have had a different conversation if I said I was going to jump a car over it.

I went back to the production company and said we could do it. They asked how much money I would need. It was the first time anyone had asked me that.

I talked to my scaffolding guy and asked what it would cost, doubled the figure and took it to them, thinking that's the last I would hear from them. But they came back and said it was a little bit dear. We haggled and came to an agreement. It was the first time I looked like getting paid the money I should have been paid for doing a stunt. In America they wouldn't think twice about paying for a stunt. In Australia the expectation had always been that I paid for it all myself.

It wasn't all rosy, though. I needed half the payment in advance to cover the cost of the scaffolding. But at the eleventh hour they said their lawyers wouldn't let them pay until they had the tapes in their hands. If anything had gone wrong I would have been forty thousand dollars in the hole.

The 'Monte Cristo' jump in June 2001 was the most technically draining and demanding I'd done because it involved a lot of set up. A week before filming we erected the scaffolding. Trying to save money, I dragooned my friends into helping. I had to be cautious and not lift scaffolding or do anything where I could be injured. If I was gone no-one else could do it and there would be a huge problem.

The ramp sat on a platform that was the equivalent of raising the ground level. The approach runway and landing ramp, almost ten metres high, required an enormous amount of scaffolding — over sixty tons. It was a lot of effort for the distance jumped but very impressive for its height and the work required. I doubt there'd been that much scaffolding in one place in Junee before. On the day of the jump a bus group turned up to visit 'Monte Cristo'. We had to make catwalks beneath the scaffolding so people could still walk around to the back of the house.

Meanwhile, I was doing rehearsal jumps in the paddock, testing the run-up, the distance to be jumped and landing on the ground. The run-up was the minimum needed to generate the right speed and I was only just getting the distance.

I had to get council permission for the jump because the landing ramp went onto council property. There was only one tree in that whole paddock, a huge gum tree, right in front of the landing ramp. At least it was something for the film crew to stand behind.

The jump itself was successful and, with ten cameras covering the event, television audiences in Australia and the United States later enjoyed it. Within an hour we were pulling down the scaffolding so as not to incur further costs. Again it was a rush, with friends and family helping to get the job done.

It was a seventy-foot jump; not the biggest but one that people talk about most. The run-bys were the worst part because I had to start slowing down at half way since there was nowhere to go unless I committed to the jump. The time I actually did the jump was the only time I got to full speed. And then there was no turning back. Even if I made a mistake I had to go with it. Being scared of heights didn't help. If a spark plug failed, a chain flew off or I missed a gear: tough. I'd either bounce off the roof and with some luck land on the ramp and cartwheel down ... or fall to my death. Footage from a camera on my helmet shows me veering off toward the edge of the ramp and then steering back to the middle.

I was more worried about people there watching me than for my own safety. Whatever happens, happens. I'm pretty resilient but I would hate it for anyone to see me get killed at a stunt. I'd hate it for anyone who loves me to see me badly injured.

You'll be right

Simone was sitting with Mum when I jumped over her house. Mum hadn't been to one of my shows since I ruptured my kidneys in 1989 but said she couldn't stay in the house when she knew I was jumping over it.

She was there that week watching the scaffolding being built alongside "Monte Cristo". It was a long way up. Of course she was thinking if I fell from that height I would be killed. Add to that the hype and this stunt scared her most of all.

Mum only knows what she sees on TV or reads about me in the papers. 'The last guy that did this was decapitated'. Or 'The last guy was burned to death', 'Five people have been killed in the Tunnel of Fire'. She doesn't know I'm wearing a fire vest. That the fire crew is there. That the tunnel is designed so that if I burst through the side I'm not going to get hung in it. Of course I don't talk about those things because people don't want to know how safe it is. They want to know how dangerous it is.

Mum was sitting there thinking, 'My God, why's he doing this!' not realising it's my job as an entertainer to sell the danger of the stunt.

Whenever I went away to perform a stunt someone had to call straight away to let her know I had made it and everything was fine. But we had to be careful. With the Tunnel of Fire at our place Mum was up in the house and a friend of the family ran up and said, 'Lawrence is okay. He's out of the tunnel. He's on fire and lying on the ground.' When I broke my ankle in 1991 Mum was in the entrance building at "Monte Cristo". One of my sisters called and told her I didn't make it but I was all right and they'd taken me away in an ambulance. Mum left another sister in charge and rushed off to Wagga Wagga.

While Mum couldn't watch my stunts, not knowing if I was going to make it or not, Dad was there every time, packing stuff on trailers and later unpacking. He backed me one hundred per cent, no matter what anybody else said. I'm quite surprised how blasé he was. The couple of times I had accidents it wasn't, 'Oh God, don't do that again!' It was, 'You'll be right; you'll be back up again. Dust yourself off.'

When I do run-bys and it feels right I just know. Sometimes I ask people how it looks. My Dad was funny. He'd say, 'I know you were going fast enough but I'll still tell you to go a little bit faster.'

'Monte Cristo', Junee, Australia's most haunted homestead and our family home.

Leaping over my family home, 'Monte Cristo'. The stunt was filmed for the US TV show, 'Stuntman's World Tour'.

Coming in to land. This jump was the tallest free-standing building to be jumped on a motorcycle at the time. Also the most haunted.

After the jump over 'Monte Cristo', with one very relieved mother, Olive Ryan.

During the run-bys when I jumped over my own house, I stopped and asked a mate, who said, 'No, I think you are going too fast.' I shouldn't have listened to him because I backed off a little and the back wheel hit the end of the landing ramp. When the bike starts pitching off the ramp you know if you have the right trajectory or not. I knew it would be close. But it was very close. It took a huge chunk out of the ramp and almost threw me off the bike.

Dad said, 'Geez, you were going too slow.'

'I realise that now.'

I turned the bike around and did it again. I couldn't leave it at that. The bike wasn't damaged. I hardly ever do two jumps but I knew I could do better. So I turned around and did it again and landed three quarters of the way down the ramp.

One day I hope to do a jump similar to the "Monte Cristo" jump but over a hot air balloon. It would be something to capture people's imaginations, like when I told people I was going to jump fifteen motorbikes with a double-decker bus. You could see their minds working: 'You mean jump fifteen buses with a motorbike?'

'No.'

'Really?'

There is a saying printed on the wall of the Junee Hotel: 'Life is not measured by the number of breaths we take but by the moments that take our breath away.' That's what it's all about; those things that astonish you.

That's what I hope it is like for people watching me because that's what it's like for me performing the stunt. It makes you feel that life's worth living. There's more to life than a monotonous daily routine.

12

THAT'S GOING TO LEAVE A MARK

In March 2003 I was preparing for a segment on the TV show *Rove Live*. Simone was on her way to 'Monte Cristo' to film some stunts with comedian Corinne Grant when she got a phone call to say I had been carted off to hospital with a broken a leg.

She was confused. I wasn't supposed to be doing anything yet. And she was right. I wasn't supposed to be doing anything. And, really, I wasn't. Not anything serious. I had just been jumping the bike over a bus for the *Rove Live* cameras as a preview for a later live cross, when I would jump a car over two double-decker buses.

Corrine Grant was going to interview me after I finished the stunt. The crew came down early and got some good footage around "Monte Cristo". After I jumped the bus I said I'd just put the bike back in the shed. On the way I did a wheel stand, flipped the bike and fell off backwards.

The next thing I knew I was lying on the ground, my leg lying in one direction and my body in another. Every time I tried to move I could lift the top part of my leg but the bottom just lay there. I had broken my femur two inches from the top of my hip joint.

People ran up and asked how I was. When I had the accident in 1991 I suspected something was wrong with my ankle. This time I knew well and truly. I'd broken the biggest bone in the body and the hardest to break. 'Yes. I've broken my leg. Call an ambulance.'

I'm very methodical. I'm not panicky. You can't panic if you want to be a good stunt person. You have to be very level headed and work well under pressure. So I was thinking, 'What's got to be done?' If I thought I could drive the ambulance, I'd have driven myself to the hospital.

I have no idea how I fell off. I can stand on the seat and do wheel stands. I can do them blindfolded, side-saddle and one-handed. This was just a normal wheel stand and it spat me off without warning. Nothing slipped or coughed; the chain didn't come off.

It messed me up pretty good. I tell people I've only broken two bones in my career: my left ankle jumping over fifteen cars (got fourteen and a half in); the other time was putting the bike back in the shed.

'You're kidding, right?'

People think that's hilarious. All these things I do and the major break came from putting the bike away.

Corinne Grant was meant to stay at 'Monte Cristo' that night. But when the *Rove Live* crew went through the carriage house Corinne, who had heard all the stories about the house, was so scared Sharon felt her fingernails in her back. When they got back to the house she asked for a cup of tea and rang a motel. 'I can't stay here. There's no way I'm staying here.'

I was in hospital for a week before I went into surgery. They had my leg pulled apart to stop the bones from clicking. I was on a good cocktail of painkillers but it still hurt like all hell, especially when I'd nod off and wake with a jolt. The day of the surgery was my thirty-second birthday; I spent my birthday having a metal rod driven through the middle of my bone. I have since seen a femur replacement on TV. They drilled a hole into the bone, drove the rod in with a hammer and screwed it down. No wonder I didn't feel so good afterwards.

A few months later *Rove Live* came back to film the stunts. I was limping around with a walking stick and someone else had to start the bike for me. We did the Wall of Fire and wheel stands and a can crush. Simone lay head-to-head with Corinne Grant with a soft drink can between them. I did a wheel stand between their heads and crushed the can. I said I had to ride closer to Simone because she wouldn't sue if I hit her.

During rehearsals for the car stunt I was starting the run-up from the carriage sheds, putting my foot down and racing toward the ramp thinking I had plenty of speed. On the night I dressed up and put my leg brace on. I hopped in the car and strapped in. Coming back from the commercial — three, two, one — I realised the brace was catching on the roll cage and I couldn't get my foot flat to the floor. I hopped out of the car, removed the brace, and finished the jump — just not with quite the speed I desired.

Tourin' in the USA

Two weeks after that, thanks to a contact on a daredevils TV show, I went to America for two months with the Mike Foster International Thrill Tour. I still needed someone to start the bike for me because I couldn't use that leg to kick-start the bike. It certainly didn't tickle when I landed.

I had only been in the country three days when I was struck down with what was first diagnosed as SARS. Thank goodness I was soon re-diagnosed with pneumonia and all I needed was some antibiotics. Then a few days later in Oregon, Illinois, we had just started a performance when we had to shelter from the effects of a nearby tornado.

The ramps we used for that stunt tour were from the fifties. Nothing had changed. No-one had thought to update to a set up that would make jumping better. It was partly the mentality that 'If it ain't broke, don't fix it'. Unfortunately, sometimes if you don't fix it things are going to break. Sometimes, when you spend all your money on the best looking gear, you have nothing left to upgrade the fundamentals.

They were so stuck in the old ways the precision driving team kept

Filming for 'Rove Live' TV show in 2003.

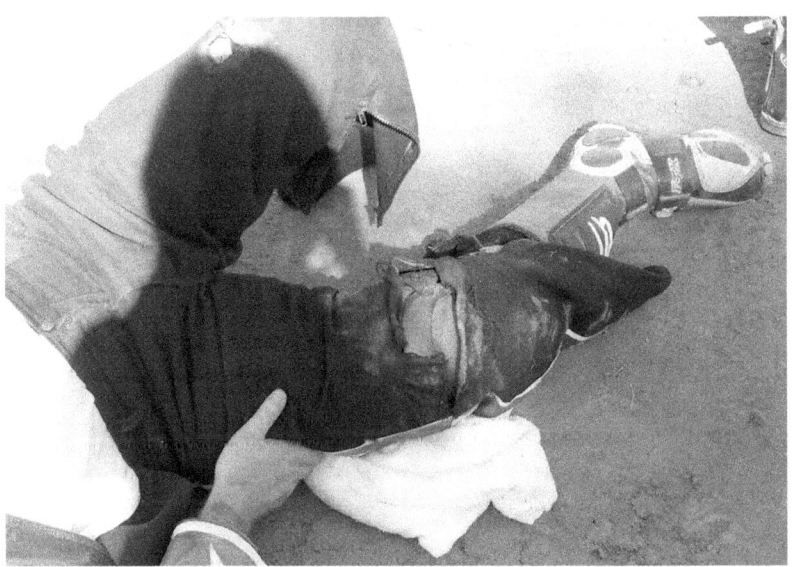

Not so straight right leg. Flipped motorcycle wheel standing. I love to tell people that in 25 years of stunt riding I have only broken two bones, and one of those was when putting the bike away.

Filming for the 'Rove Live' TV show in 2003. Three months after the broken right femur we were back to finish filming.

A place where people can come to see the real heroes of the silver screen and daredevils of the fair grounds who risked their lives to entertain people around the world.

one arm out the window, supposedly showing how skilful they were to need only one hand to perform the manoeuvres. I thought, 'A. You look like a bit of a clown. B. It's not a good practice to let people think that you can be a good driver using one hand. You need both hands.'

It's only now with the action sports, the free style motocross and rally cars that they are using progression ramps, or scooped ski ramps, which are easier on the cars and bikes. They are working out that, with suspension, by adjusting the gas in the shock absorbers you can make the car launch and fly better. Certainly the sponsorship from energy drink companies helps. Yet while sponsored drivers have the budget to afford ramps built with the best materials and technology, they usually just go for distance and forget the spectacle or impression created by a line of buses. That's what they are losing.

A few of the modern breed will be remembered; those like Travis Pastrana, the American stunt performer who multi-tasks in supercross, motocross and rally racing, and has a good branding image. When kids come to the Stuntman and Daredevil Hall of Fame they might see Travis and their parents or grandparents will be able to say, 'That's what Evel Knievel was like in my day.'

Due to the sheer number of people in the United States there are more things happening for stunt performers. Even though many of the performers face the same struggles, and are living out of vans, their presentation is glossier and their media presence makes them look bigger and better.

When I toured there jumping bikes in 2003, there was much more fanfare than for stunt shows in Australia. There were people with flags cheering us on and everyone wanted to talk to me. They thought I was special, even though I wasn't really. They were attracted to me because I was different. I did more shows in two months there than I did in a whole year in Australia. But unless I had someone there to look after me, market me, and look after my gear when I wasn't there, I couldn't keep doing it.

In each town we appeared at perhaps only a thousand people would show up but they thought that was a huge success. In that respect it was much easier. Another Australian stunt performer made a good living doing stunts with four-wheel bikes in the UK. The towns were close together and he attracted good crowds. But he was frustrated when he returned to Australia because there were fewer opportunities and people weren't interested.

The doctors told me to keep off my leg and I was still getting treatment a year after my accident. A sports therapist told me I should have started using it as soon as I could. My recovery was so slow that a doctor said I would always have a limp. Once I started receiving the correct treatment my leg was nearly as good as new. But the doctors continued to scare me by saying I shouldn't have another accident because the rod would bend. And rods are extremely hard to get out when they are bent. Good to know.

That accident led to me doing more car stunts. The heavy impact of coming down from jumps on the bike was quite painful for the first few years. It made me rethink things. If there was a reason for me having that accident perhaps it was to slow me down. I thought, 'I'm breaking a bone for what? For a bit of exposure? For nothing. It wasn't worth it.'

I had exhausted bike jumping, unless I could jump further or higher than some other guys. I would move on to cars. With younger guys coming onto the scene doing backflips and tricks, I was stepping away at the right time. People watching me doing daredevil stunts wouldn't have understood the difference.

The spooky side story to my femur break was that it happened where, many years before, a boy was thrown from a horse and killed at 'Monte Cristo'.

13
GUINNESS WORLD RECORDS

A Guinness World Record is not the same thing as a world record, yet a Guinness World Record means more, has more allure, to the average person. Even if I have ten world records, people want to know about the two Guinness Records.

Guinness Records can be very quirky and it's easier than you might think to set one. Guinness World Records is more interested in how many marshmallows were in the tub of jelly jumped with a motorbike than the distance of the jump. They are more interested in the images that will sell their book.

After I broke my leg I had been learning two-wheel driving, sporadically having a go myself, but no-one was there to teach me. I didn't understand the balance points, that the fuel would run out of the carburettors as I tipped up the cars and they would stall, or that the little wheel on the side would get in the way.

Adjustments have to be made for a two-wheeling car. If it's not fuel injected it needs to have the float set higher so there is more fuel in the fuel bowl of the carburettor and it doesn't starve for fuel. The fuel pumps need to be in tip top condition and the tank needs to be full so fuel can be picked up even when the car leans.

Sometimes you have to be careful because the oil won't circulate. The Toyota Corolla that I was driving was the last of the rear-wheel drive Corollas. Rear-wheel drive cars are much easier to two-wheel than front-wheel drive cars because front wheel drives are pulling along as you steer and it's easier for it to slip out. And the Corolla engine leans the right way in the engine bay, which has the effect of straightening it up. The trainer wheel on the side works best near the front door pillar, where the main weight of the car is. On tight turns it is more of a hindrance than a help because it gets in the way.

I spoke to some other stunt people to learn about these things but they wouldn't show me. It was like a magician's secret.

Then I saw an article about a guy in Melbourne who taught defensive driving courses. It mentioned that he drove on two wheels in a little Toyota Corolla. I rang him but at first he wasn't interested. He'd had many such calls from people who fancied themselves but wanted to learn for free. I said I knew the fundamentals and just needed someone to take me the extra step. He tried to put me off, saying it would cost a few thousand dollars to cover expenses like the hire of the track. I said yes, not knowing where I'd get the money.

He made me pay in advance, I went down to Melbourne and he had the car set up with a good rig. I watched him do it first and thought he wasn't doing it very smoothly — he started off at an odd angle and swung the car sharply as he stood it up off the ramp — but I figured that must be the way it was done. His lesson was basically to put me in the car and point me at the ramp, with bits and pieces of advice when it wasn't working out.

I have since tried to teach other people the techniques of two-wheeling and it is difficult to relay the message to the driver. It does come down to trial and error.

His ramp, though, was set at a funny angle towards a wall. I would almost have the car on two wheels but ran out of space because of the wall. When I asked if I could point the ramp down the straight he said it wouldn't work because I had to hook the car to stand it up. But I said I'd have more chance to 'chase' the car as it stood up if I had more room.

Within four attempts I was two-wheeling. Within an hour I was two-wheeling down the straight at Calder Park Thunderdome and by the end of the day I could go right around the track. He pointed me in the right direction and in the end it came naturally to me. He said he'd never taught anyone to do it in such a short time. Half the day was usually spent just getting people to line up the ramp. I'd obviously done a lot of that.

The trouble I had was forgetting my motorbike wheel standing, which required that I was on and off the gas to keep the bike up on its back wheel. I was trying to do the same thing with the car — but I didn't need to, it balanced differently; I had to keep the gas steady.

I was sore and sorry for myself at the end of that day because my arms and shoulders had to fight the wheel.

Through the gap

My instructor must have been impressed because he asked me to come to be a driving instructor with him. He was involved in a Hyundai launch, where the manufacturer came with all its cars and PR people. We demonstrated two-wheeling in a Toyota; just a bit of fun for the occasion.

After that I asked if I could take measurements of the ramps and car so I could set one up at home and keep practising. He said I could just take the car, which I did, making an exact copy so we had two cars and I could practise whenever I wanted.

I built my own tar track so I could practise every day.

Six months later Guinness World Records approached me to do a two-wheeling stunt. They had a formula for two-wheeling through the narrowest gap: subtracting the height of the car from the width of the gap. I thought if they were coming down to film me I should make the most of the opportunity and set two world records, the second being for the most people in the car while two-wheeling.

I asked the local council to use a road built for a new subdivision, got all my friends to come down and hop in the car with safety helmets and glasses, and practised.

I was still using the rig with a little training wheel so the car wouldn't be damaged if it toppled. It was purely a psychological thing. I had never needed it but I had never driven without it. If I took it off I'd know it wasn't there and my mind would start playing tricks with me.

And that's what happened. Guinness came to Junee in July 2005 and wanted me take the rig off. One of my friends said, 'You'll be right. You've done this hundreds of times without that wheel on, haven't you?'

'Of course I have ...'

As soon as I took the rig off I was over-cautious and had trouble getting the car to stand up. It took half a dozen attempts but I eventually got it. The weight of the people on board — equal to the weight of the car — made it strenuous to drive and the weight in the back lifted the front, so steering was light and I was chasing more than I would have liked. We did three runs all the way down the road and I got the Guinness record — eight people on board.

Then we had to do the gap.

We got the gap quite small and I was feeling confident, having taken my friends with me to break the other record. And this time I didn't have to worry about hurting anyone. I was about to try to narrow the gap again and the Guinness people told me I couldn't do any further.

'What do you mean?'

'Because this is to be listed for the first time in Guinness World Records, we can't make it so that no-one can break it. You have to set it so someone else has a chance to break the world record.' The problem with that was you could leave it open and the next person could come along and take it down to the finest detail. It would be impossible to break.

And that is what has happened. My record was for driving a 1985 Toyota Corolla on two wheels through a gap eighty centimetres wider

Filming for the live morning TV show, 'Sunrise', with Grant Denyer.

Balancing act. A test run before taking reporter Grant Denyer for a drive on two wheels.

Guinness World Records. This was my second record as my original record was broken a year before. (Note Grant Denyer's autograph).

Grant Denyer, reporter, daredevil, race car driver and game show host.

than the height of the car. Since then I have lost it and broken it and lost it again to someone driving between two poles, which is easier than driving between two cars. Now people try to break it by tying their shock absorbers up so the wheels won't spring out when the car leaves the ramp. I saw that tactic when I went to China in 2012.

It was a huge thing getting the record for the first time. It made the front page of the local paper and everyone wanted to know about it. I was invited to the TV studio when they broadcast the record attempt, which meant I could receive not just the usual certificates but also be presented with a medal for each record. I wasn't expecting that but they yanked me out of line on the way in and made me up so I could be interviewed on camera.

TV host Grant Denyer — also a V8 Supercar driver and a bit of a daredevil — was hosting the Guinness World Records show. I was his first interview subject when he started out as a reporter with Prime7 News in Wagga Wagga.

I know plenty of stunt performers with ten or twelve Guinness Records but I'm still proud of those two medals. I know it's not hard to get a Guinness Record but my two-wheeling records were significant for me. It was a personal challenge. That's how I see things. If it doesn't challenge me I'm usually not interested.

I have a huge collection of Guinness World Records books, right back to the small books before they had pictures in them. I'm missing five of the earliest books but have the rest to the present day. They will make a great display in the Stuntman and Daredevil Hall of Fame.

14

You're a Hero

I love any action movie and am very much taken by superheroes. I think that's the ultimate cool.

Batman was my favourite superhero because he didn't have any special powers; he just had great gadgets. I made a utility belt and tried to make grappling hooks. I thought if I was going to be a real superhero Batman was as close as I could get. I love the whole idea of Bruce Wayne being Batman.

We toyed with the idea of a comic strip with me as an action hero. I have some frames of the character hanging on the wall of my office. The alter ego of Lawrence Legend (stunt driver during the day and crime fighter at night) is millionaire Lance Langfield.

In 2008 I became a real hero — not a superhero but a Toyota V6 HiLux Hero.

While I was two-wheeling, doing twenty-minute shows, I was still doing occasional work at the driving school, coaching defensive driving and offering Stunt Driver for a Day experiences. We built small jump ramps so people could get a sense of the thrill of jumping. They learned how to do reverse spins and handbrake turns and, at the end of the day, we would take them on a two-wheel drive.

We were doing that at Oran Park Raceway when two guys turned up to watch. The instructor knew them and talked to them about the two-wheeling. That day I was in the car doing spins, suffering from motion sickness. I got out saying I'd throw up if we didn't swap. I started two-wheeling in front of the guys who I later learned owned the Drift Australian series and had just bought cars and ramps from the Holden Driving Team.

The driving team had been doing the circuit for years but Holden had withdrawn its sponsorship. The new owners were looking for a sponsor so they could relaunch the precision driving show at fairs. They were still looking for a two-wheeler driver and within a week they called to ask if I would help them set up a two-wheeling car.

They gave me a brand new Toyota HiLux to take home and cut up. I fixed it up within a week and had it two-wheeling around my track. I sent them some video footage and they asked me to do another one. They flew down a few of the former Holden drivers to complete the team but asked if I would do the two-wheeling to start the show.

None of them knew me well because they were all rally drivers and I was a stunt driver. I thought they just wanted me to fill in until they learned how to two-wheel. A couple of them had two-wheeled before but they weren't very good at it — they could only go one way around the track.

When it came time to take publicity photos they wanted me in the picture. I said I was only filling in and it wouldn't be appropriate to be in their publicity shots. But they insisted and it suddenly became clear they wanted me in the team ... without telling me.

I was reluctant. The team was always only four drivers, one of whom would swap cars to do the two-wheeling. I was driver number five. The fifth wheel. But I could two-wheel without the safety rig for the publicity shots and they wanted me in the team.

Best in the business

According to their own publicity, the Toyota V6 HiLux Heroes consisted of five of Australia's top motorsport drivers (including me: 'one of the best in the business'). The team performed in front of millions of people in Australia every year — at major shows, motorsport events and trade days — with a variety of stunts and formation driving. Members of the team were experienced in rallying, drifting, motorkhanas (manoeuvring a car through tight tests as quickly as possible), dirt circuit racing and stunt work.

Highlights in the act included balancing a HiLux on two wheels and a twelve metre ramp-to-ramp jump. Other stunts were drifting, nose-to nose driving, reverse handbrake turn flicks, a range of vehicle jumping displays and high-speed crossovers, where four of the vehicles were driven towards each other in an X formation.

My favourite part of being a V6 HiLux Heroes driver — according to my team profile — was 'entertaining crowds in all parts of Australia and getting to drive a near-standard HiLux ute on two wheels'. My favourite stunt during the show was, no surprise, two-wheel driving: 'I get to see the places we perform at from some interesting angles!'

I might have been a highlight but all I did was help clean cars, set up ramps and sit around for fifteen minutes before I did my minute or so of two-wheeling around the track.

We performed around two or three shows on one hundred and twenty days each year. We were busy.

After a show the other guys would stand around talking about the old times with the Holden team and how good they were, how they cornered sideways, how close they were to one another — jocks with their pants down talking about how big they were. I had never been around anything like that before.

The first show I did was at Kiama, where the oval was on a cliff — very picturesque. I was setting up a ramp near the edge and one the drivers asked me what I was doing.

'That's where I'm going to two-wheel.'

'That's really close to the rail. You can't two-wheel there.'

'Well this is where the track is; where do you want me to two-wheel?'

'You'll never be able to get it up there without running into the fence.'

'We'll just see about that.'

He walked off, throwing his hands in the air, and shook his head. I two-wheeled right around the edge.

I had some good times with the Toyota team. I got to perform at some of the bigger royal shows that I didn't get to do on my motorbikes. A special occasion came in the first year during the Sydney Royal Easter Show. Our appearance fell on my birthday and everyone in the arena joined the commentator singing Happy Birthday to me as I two-wheeled around.

Another thing I liked about the HiLux Heroes was that, as a kid growing up and watching the Holden Driving Team at the Wagga Wagga Show, I always thought it would be cool to do that, even though my main interest was in motorbikes (and in *crashing* the cars).

Because I did two-wheeling the team used me for promotional events; any time there were news cameras they had me two-wheeling to camera.

While I was gaining their respect, I also felt I was being pushed away. They wanted to make me a full member of the team and tried to get me doing precision driving. I could do it but was never comfortable driving at a hundred kilometres an hour, sideways next to a fence where there were heaps of people. I was competent but they weren't confident and retained me as a fifth member.

I am only half joking when I say the reason I was kept away from the formation driving was because they were afraid I would hit them. The boss always said if there were an accident with the formation team he would send me to crash into them; if they were going to wreck four cars they might as well wreck five.

I met many interesting people with the HiLux Heroes and there were lots of laughs. One bonus early on was Toyota paying for us to have a nice dinner and watch a State of Origin rugby league match; they bought us Queensland and NSW jerseys and put us in good seats to watch the game.

I got to do two-wheeling demonstrations in Sydney's Olympic

Park before a *Top Gear* live show. I took people for rides and tried to teach Formula One Toyota driver Timo Glock during a promotional day at Calder Raceway. I also showed former Grand Prix motorcycle rider Daryl Beattie and Greg Rust, motor racing commentator on motorsports TV program *RPM*, how to two-wheel.

We travelled to places like Cairns, staying in tropical resorts and hanging out beside the pool when we weren't performing. While it was an exciting time, I was also lonely. I would rather have had someone there to share the experience.

Travelling so much meant we also didn't eat properly. We'd finish late and go to a pub or a pizza place. All the guys drank. I got on all right with them but I didn't drink and felt like a fish out of water.

There was pressure in the job outside the arena. I have never washed so many cars in my life. After every performance we had to clean the cars. Mine hardly ever got dirty but theirs did because they were flying around in the mud. Wash them, shammy them down, tie them onto the trucks. It was very much a showy's life: perform, pack up, go to the next place. Some shows were back to back, occasionally three in a row, keeping us away from home for four weeks.

If you were young and single, without the ties of a home, it would be an ideal job. There were lots of road trips and interstate flights; lots of time sitting in airports. One of the older guys had been with the Holden team for twenty years or more. When he had enough of it he worked out he had spent two years of his life living in Sydney. His home was in Queensland.

Not what it seems

The fun times were overshadowed by the drama of working in a team. I don't seem to be a team player. It was like being in school: kids puffing up and acting tough — all bravado and machismo.

I also learned to be more ruthless. Stunt work is a business and has

Toyota V6 HiLux Heroes. Two wheel driving or 'high skiing' as it's called in the USA.

Taking a reporter for a drive for live TV.

Publicity stunt with Toyota Formula One driver, Timo Glock (Melbourne, 2008).

Thumbs up from Timo Glock after being taken two wheel driving.

to be treated as such. The bosses there were cut-throat. They would go out of their way to create hell for competing entertainers. I was small fry compared to them; they could wipe me out in a heartbeat. They were always keen to let me know how expendable I was. When they started quibbling over travelling allowances I wondered what I was doing there.

The Toyota V6 HiLux Heroes were losing their lustre.

I was calling home saying I was homesick. We were constantly on the road, away for three or four days at a time, and the royal shows required us to be away two weeks in a row. I didn't feel comfortable with the other guys. Mostly they treated me fine but I didn't feel included.

Because I had the fifth car that didn't fit on the truck I had to drive it myself. They wanted me to clean up their ramps but wouldn't lend a hand to pick up the two-wheeling ramps. If there was an opportunity to leave me out they would.

It was a little bit awkward and after two and a half years I had had enough. I sensed they would phase me out and after some very difficult driving at the Bathurst Show I made my decision.

In previous years they had let me miss the last day of the Adelaide Show so I could join my family at the 'Monte Cristo' Ball. But at dinner after the Bathurst Show they told me I had to stay until the end of the Adelaide Show. I packed up my gear, drove home and rang up the next day and said, 'I quit.'

It was a good experience but I didn't regret leaving. I'd never take it back but I wish I'd left in happier circumstances.

People thought it must have been a dream job; it must have been ideal. The driving team had headhunted me. They knew I had Guinness Records driving a Toyota and the sponsor for the Toyota HiLux Heroes was interested in what I did and used Lawrence Legend to introduce their first promotional video. It was regular money. But it wasn't what it seemed.

Nor were things on the home front.

While I was happy to get out of touring with the HiLux Heroes, my wife at the time wasn't so thrilled to have me home. It ruined her social life. I had been away from home for long periods over several years and my wife had found ways to entertain herself.

We had married in 1997. I met her through a dating agency. It sounds embarrassing looking back on it but I never went to pubs or places where I was likely to meet a partner. I never had much luck with romance and usually tried to keep away from girls. The only girls who were interested in me were the tattooed rebellious type who thought I must be tough and hard living because I was a bike-riding daredevil.

I went out with a girl when I was seventeen; her parents knew Sharon's parents before Sharon and Charlie were married and they used to hang around with Charlie and me at 'Monte Cristo'. In those days I wasn't doing real stunts. People just thought I was doing boys' things, mucking around in the paddock.

After that girls seemed to think I was the kind of bloke they could chase to upset dad. I am so far from the stereotypical rebel. I did my fair share of things I wasn't supposed to do but I certainly wasn't a law-breaking vandal or someone who'd spend his time in the corner of a bar smoking and getting drunk.

When I got older I only wanted a family.

Separation was inevitable once I found out where my wife's interests lay but we stuck it out for another year. The divorce wasn't easy — a lot of *he said, she said* — but it led to a period of personal reflection and consideration of some of the deeper, more meaningful and spiritual aspects to life.

I took a break from stunts to focus on my family and take on more responsibility at 'Monte Cristo'.

I always had a good relationship with my parents. My Dad was my real hero. He always had faith in me, no matter what I wanted to do. He believed in me. I'm trying to offer the same support to my sons.

15
AN ANGEL APPEARS

When I separated from my wife I lost all faith in intimate relationships. I didn't want to deal with women again. I was burnt badly. I had no interest. Women, I thought, can make or break you; the time you spend focusing on them you could be spending on your goals, your career or the rest of your life.

A friend who was a medium helped me through those hard times, letting me know there was a light at the end of the tunnel. 'Keep strong,' she said. 'Don't worry about what's happening now; it will sort itself out.'

She also said, 'There's someone coming to meet you.'

'No, I'm not interested. I don't care if they are a messenger from God, I'm not interested.'

Within days I met Sophia at 'Monte Cristo'.

Sophia's home was in Temora, sixty kilometres away. One day she had to take her daughter to Wagga Wagga. On the way home her daughter said she wanted to come through 'Monte Cristo'. She had heard about it at school.

They pulled up and came into the entrance building, where I was waiting to greet visitors. She looked at me, looked away and looked back again. She caught my attention with her fiery red hair. She thought I had a familiar face, as though she had known me somewhere before. She even thought my voice sounded familiar.

She asked when 'Monte Cristo' was open and I reeled off the opening hours but she said she didn't want to go through until she came back with her son.

They returned the following Saturday and were on the doorstep at ten o'clock. The kids were eager and raced in before her. Dad was behind the desk and spoke to them. I walked in after they got their tickets.

'Oh, you decided to come back!'

She hesitated, 'Yes, the kids wanted to come.'

They went to the front door of the house and the kids rang the doorbell. I went in a side entrance and answered the door for them. Sophia's feeling that I was somehow familiar grew stronger.

'I know you,' she thought. 'How do I know you?'

I showed them where to go and followed them around. While they were in the boys' bedroom I noticed Sophia's son was wearing a bright red Honda shirt. We started up a conversation about motorbikes. Sophia was very timid, very quiet, and just listened to me talking to her son.

From there they went to the balcony at the front of the house. Sophia says she found it calming and peaceful. It felt like home.

I left them and they walked around the balcony to the side stairs and down behind the house to the ballroom, where antiques were for sale. The kids went straight to a huge cat sitting on one of the chairs. I soon found them there and said, 'That's my cat, Beau.' Again the kids talked with me while Sophia stood back and watched.

They went out onto the lawn and I talked to them more about the haunted house and about mediums and psychic people. I asked if they had heard about that sort of thing. I said I wanted to tell them a story. The kids listened intently as I told them about a medium who said that one day a lady with red hair and two children would come to 'Monte Cristo'. I would meet her and she would have an answer for me.

The children listened with wide eyes and open mouths.

Sophia looked on puzzled. It was all a bit much.

When Sophia and the kids went back to the entrance building, I was waiting there with Dad. The children bought some souvenirs. Sophia still said nothing and took the kids to the car. By the time she got in the front seat I had caught up with her and offered her my business card. I was nervous.

'If you can remember what that answer is can you give me a call?'

The card had my name, a picture of a car up on two wheels and the Lawrence Legend email address. She didn't know what it meant. She closed the door and sat there while the kids asked what had happened.

She knew she couldn't leave until she had gone back and talked to me. She put the windows down and asked the kids to wait for five minutes. Dad was still behind the desk in the entrance building and Sophia asked if she could speak to me.

'Of course you can, love. I'll just get him for you.' He walked up to the house and told me a lady in the entrance building wanted to speak to me.

I walked in looking a bit shocked. 'Oh, hello there.'

'Hi, I think I have something I need to tell you.'

She started to talk but I said we'd better have the conversation outside. When we were out the front I asked, 'What is it?'

'I have been to a medium and she told me I was going to meet somebody with salt and pepper hair, the most amazing blue eyes and he would be someone I'd make a major impact on for the rest of my life.'

I just looked at her. My eyes got bigger and I offered my hand and said, 'Hello, my name is Lawrence.'

She reached out, 'Hello, my name is Sophia.'

From that day on we kept in contact, we emailed each other, we phoned each other. Sophia's phone bill got to fifteen hundred dollars

— cheap therapy. It was hours and hours of talking about anything and everything. Things about the hairdressing business she was thinking of opening, major decisions she needed to make; she had a bad experience in the past year but was trusting me with things she said she'd never trusted with anyone.

The relationship blossomed. I asked her to come on one of the ghost tours and introduced her to Mum and Dad. And to the house. I came out of my shell and she saw me morph from shy and withdrawn Lawrence into showman Lawrence; Lawrence with a direct voice, confident about his subject matter: 'Monte Cristo'.

That's what sealed it, she says.

You can't help but like her
We realised we had lived the same lives with different people. The similarity was uncanny, from ex-partners' first names and last names, what they did for a living, how we were treated. It was as though the Universe was trying to line us up but didn't quite get it right.

When we started seeing each other, going out for coffee, I was reluctant. It was almost as though we were having an affair. I didn't want people to think I'd left one relationship and found someone else on the rebound. I'm a private person and was trying to keep what was happening secret even while I was fighting it.

We could just be friends. I wasn't interested in a relationship. They all end in tears. I don't want to go through that rubbish again.

No matter how much I fought it and tried to protect my children's feelings, our friendship was revealed and people said, 'Don't you think it's a bit soon?' My ex-wife was engaged by that stage so my moving on was slow by comparison.

Since then Sophia has moved to Junee and purchased land behind my block, with a gate linking our properties. Sophia said she felt she

One of our first dates (left). And (right) lunch in China during Guinness World Records filming. Sophia had never travelled so much until she met me.

Sophia watches her first ever live stunt performance: a jumping stunt car for radio promotion in Cunberra.

The thing that makes us feel free and happy: riding the Harley-Davidson.

truly belonged at 'Monte Cristo'. Mum and Dad were very welcoming and treated her like one of their daughters.

Sophia coming along was an opportunity for me to rethink my life. She changed my outlook. I realised that, even though my stunt work was my passion, if I wasn't enjoying it, what was the point?

She grounded me, kept me looking forward; if you surround yourself with positive people you can only go forward, you can't go backwards. She's the one who says, 'Don't listen to people. You do what you believe in. I can see a bright future for you. You need to keep going the way you are going.'

That, and the loss of my Dad, has made me more determined. Where would I be if it wasn't for my Dad all those years ago saying, 'Lawrence, you can be whatever you want to be in life … It doesn't matter if you don't become the best but you need to set a goal for yourself and try.'

I feel comforted and reassured when I see people achieve great things. It makes me feel good. I think that's how people *should* feel when anyone does something well. That's why I push negative people out of my life, as much as I can. You can't let people of ill will affect you. Don't let negative people rent space in your head, the saying goes; put the rent up and kick them out.

Sophia is a huge part of that. She had to witness three years of my ups and downs; going through a divorce and estrangement from my children. She's been there to support me. I certainly wouldn't be where I am now if it wasn't for her. I'm very grateful she's in my life.

I have fun with Sophia's kids and can usually make them smile if they are down. Being a teenager often isn't the best time of your life; with hormones working their little tricks it can be depressing, so why not do what you can to cheer them along? Children didn't ask to be brought into this world. We brought them here and we should give them as many opportunities as we can.

When children come to 'Monte Cristo' I connect with them straight away. I have fun with them and tell them what I have learned, that you can do whatever you want as long as you believe. If you can believe in yourself and believe that anything is possible you can do it. If I can say those words in a way that a child can understand, I can provide the confidence and self-belief they need.

I'm pretty good with kids because I'm just a big kid. I like to remind people that immaturity is the word boring people use to describe fun people. I can be an embarrassment sometimes but if it makes people laugh it's worth it.

Sophia and I are both good at reading people. We pick up on things that other people don't realise. She is a people person. She was a hairdresser for many years and knows how to talk to people. She calls it a counselling job: only ten per cent of it is cutting hair, the other ninety per cent is helping to solve people's problems or listening as they get some difficulty off their chest.

Otherwise, Sophia had lived a sheltered life. She hadn't seen many movies. And, even though she had lived nearby, she had no idea who I was. That meant she came with no pre-conceived idea of who I was and took me on my merits.

She knows I get angry when I see someone else being hurt emotionally. My protective instincts come out. I get angry but don't want to show that anger to the person who is being hurt. I'd rather take control of that situation and stop it from happening. If I can show some kindness, offer my time and listen, I might be able to feel what they feel.

Sophia's a gentle person. A softer energy. I'm more forceful. If I care for someone, I want to show that love. Actions speak louder than words.

Not only did Sophia not know who Lawrence Legend was, she also didn't know who Evel Knievel was; so I had to introduce her to my library for some remedial education. After long sessions of video indoctrination, she now knows that Evel Knievel was a daring cycle jumper, a veteran of hundreds of successful death-defying leaps over cars, trucks and buses; a veteran, too, of failed leaps, leaps that no-one else was game to try; he devoted years of practice and study to the dangerous sport of cycle jumping; he had the strength and courage to go on after suffering many serious injuries; his is a story of grit and determination, courage and a willingness to face uncertain odds; above all, his is 'a story of the undaunted faith of one man in his ability to shape his own, unique destiny.'

Sophia thinks there may be some similarities.

The first stunt of mine that Sophia saw was for an FM radio station in Canberra. I had to run a car up a ramp, through a Ring of Fire and land on fifteen cars, parked side by side. Whichever car I landed on was the lucky number in a bingo game.

Sophia remembers that stunt well because of the nerves and sickness she experienced. She was white with shock that I was actually going to do it. She looked at me and looked at the car and looked at me again, imagining the car flipping and trapping me underneath. She didn't want me to get hurt.

As usual, I was pumped with adrenalin. She had never seen me like that, with my eyes full of determination: this is what I am doing, I'm going to do it, I'm going to do it well, I can't wait to do it, nothing is going to stop me.

After the build up for the stunt everything went silent. Sophia could see the car. She could see the ramp. She could see me revving the car and then no-one could breathe. She could only watch and listen and see what would happen. She says when I got out of the car she was very relieved. I was clearly happy, like I was walking on a cloud. I talked non-stop for the radio station.

From then on Sophia was less fearful about my stunts. She could see what drove me to do my work. It was a part of me; how I had been made. And she could see where that determination came from.

'Reg,' she said, 'was the most motivated man I've ever met. He had obstacles put in front of him his whole life and he told me that no matter what they were or how big they were, or even if they seemed the worst things possible, he could always turn them around and make them into a positive. He understood they were put there for a reason; they were put there for him to work harder to get to where he wanted.'

That's what Dad had done and that is what I am doing.

16

MADE IN CHINA

In October 2012, on a Tuesday morning in the frozen foods section in the supermarket with Sophia, my mobile phone rang. When I answered a deep voice with a heavy Chinese accent asked, 'Is this Lawrence Ryan?'

The voice said he was from Guinness World Records and he got my phone number from Guinness World Records in London.

He told me he ran a special show in China once a year and asked if I would be interested in coming to two-wheel and attempt to regain my smallest gap record. The show was the Guinness World Records Special for Zheng Da Zong Yi, a prime time series in Beijing that had been running for almost twenty years. Several episodes of the show were dedicated to Guinness World Records. They invited record holders from all over the world to perform their stunts in the studio. Outdoor records had to be pre-recorded.

It caught me off guard. I was just doing my shopping.

I said, sure, but when would they want me.

'Very soon. Very soon.' He asked for my email address.

Sophia looked at me wondering who could be on the phone because I was talking very strangely and then spelling out my name slowly; not because he couldn't understand me but because I had trouble understanding his accent and it took some time for me to be confident he had taken down the address correctly.

When I got off the phone I said, 'You're never going to believe this. That fellow was from China. He knows all about me. They want me to go to China and do some stunt work.'

'Don't be silly.'

'No, I'm serious. They want me to go to China.'

We grabbed the last few things on our shopping list and hurried home. The email message was there but it was from a Hotmail account and I immediately suspected someone was scamming me.

Nevertheless, I emailed back and said I'd be interested.

They said they'd need me there the next week. What would I need?

I thought, 'What!' But answered that I'd obviously need a car, preferably with rear-wheel drive and other particulars.

They said they had a car and sent me a photo of the Chinese-built Chery car. Chinese cars are left-hand drive. I said I was only proficient driving two-wheels with right-hand drive and they had to lock the diff up so both wheels turned at the same time. I'd need extra spare tyres because the surfaces I usually drove on ripped the tyres up.

How could they get this organised in time?

They said it wouldn't be a problem.

Then things started to click. They already had a right-hand drive car? Something was going on. I pushed a bit and asked why they didn't get someone else to come, perhaps the guy who now had the record? They said they had already asked him and he declined. The guy who tied his shock absorber up to break the record didn't want to perform in front of a live audience for someone else's television show.

They said they would pay for me to go over and they'd pay me for performing the stunt. I said yes but, thinking of Sophia, I wouldn't go by myself. At first they refused so I said in that case I wouldn't do it. Then they agreed but the additional airfare would come out of my fee. I said fine, thinking it was just for a few days and it would be a wonderful experience to do some two-wheeling in China, even if I didn't break the record.

That was Tuesday. The flight to China was on Sunday evening.

I had to drive to Sydney early on Thursday to drop off our passports to a visa agent so our visas would be processed in time. I'd already downloaded and completed the paperwork using the information I'd received from the TV company in China but when I turned up in the agent's office I had to start again.

There were too many red flags for the red bureaucracy.

Instead of staying at the Media Centre in Beijing I was staying at the Hilton in Beijing. I was no longer visiting the Guinness World Records representative at a television studio; I was going to his 'work'.

I paid the extra fee to rush the application through and was told I had to pick it up at four the next day.

Meanwhile, I had to drive back to Junee for a meeting. On Friday I asked my uncle in Penrith to go into the Sydney CBD to collect our passports. He took them home and our friend Darren, who lived in Minchinbury, drove to Penrith to pick them up. On Sunday morning we drove to Sydney airport and he met us on the motorway to give us our passports.

Overwhelmed

Within five days of taking that call in a supermarket in Junee I was on a plane to China with Sophia. And in that time I had to drag out my cars — front wheel drive and rear wheel drive — and practise two-wheeling because I hadn't two-wheeled for nearly a year. I just hoped it was like riding a bike and I wouldn't forget.

I had no idea what the Chinese car was like, if I would be able to two-wheel it or what else would be involved. I gave them measurements for a ramp I needed.

We flew into China, landed, changed flights and early in the morning ended up in Beijing, where a lanky, young Chinese guy met us holding an iPad with our names on it. He took us to a hotel near the airport. After thirteen hours flying we had less than three hours sleep before we were taken back to the airport and flew another four hours to where I was to perform.

There we met the owner of the twenty-strong Chinese stunt team — they called him 'Coach'. Only after our flights were booked did they tell me I would be competing against two of them, stunt drivers Hua and Chun Lin.

Sophia thought it was amazing. We were totally ignorant about the culture. And the food. We were awed by the scale of the cities and how people lived. It was overwhelming.

Most of our communication once we arrived was by sign language.

We were taken to an urban area near Guangzhou. It looked deserted. There were lots of buildings but no traffic and no people. Filming was to take place in a huge trucking complex with lots of beautiful, smooth concrete. When we arrived there we met the stunt team — men and women. Our interpreter showed me the car — the only right-hand Chery in China, they told me — and asked if I wanted to practise. 'More pressure,' I thought, 'Thank you very much!'

I asked if they had locked up the gear box for me. They said no. I was surprised. Normally you have to take the engine out; it's a big job. But they said they had the car prepared. Instead, they had disconnected all the brakes except for the wheel that was in the air. When I went off the ramp and put my foot on the brake it would lock that one wheel by itself leaving the other wheel to turn on the ground. I had never done that before. 'You want me to go off the ramp in a manual car and as soon as I leave the ramp put my foot on the brake to lock the wheel, use my other foot for the gas and concentrate on my two-wheeling?'

'Yes.'

'I'll give it a go; what can I lose?'

They said they'd fix it if they needed to. I thought that was a big call but they had lots of people to draw on if work had to be done.

The venue was set out nicely. There were barricades everywhere and hundreds of beautiful shiny trucks parked off to one side.

I got in the car and told our interpreter I would probably need to go off the ramp twenty times before I could two-wheel, just to get the feel of the car. It was all very new to me. I got in the car. Warmed it up and thought, 'Here we go.'

And I was off the ramp, straight up, two-wheeling. First go.

When I went off the ramp I put my foot on the brake, which was not a natural reaction, but I worked out if I put it on harder I could get more grip on the wheel. It was a brilliant idea. I had never thought of this concept. Normally to two-wheel for a television commercial you would need to modify the car so heavily it was practically ruined. But disconnecting the brakes was simple — though not very good if you were going in a straight line and wanted to stop in a hurry.

I two-wheeled down, turned around and came back. The Coach came over and shook my hand and joked through the interpreter: 'You said it would take many attempts. You lied. We will have to worry now!'

I spent two hours in a brand new car doing donuts and handbrake turns and spinning it and having a wow of a time on the concrete. Sophia, taking photographs, stood out like … a red head in the middle of a crowd of people with black hair. All the girls came and spoke to her and pointed to her hair, saying how pretty it was.

We had lunch in a beautiful restaurant with the film crew and the guide who looked after us. Sophia was impressed that they treated us with such respect, like a king and queen. The guide ordered our food and we learned that what we call 'Chinese food' and what real Chinese food is are totally different. First they asked if I wanted a drink. So

Practising for the Guinness World Records in China.

Having a break between rehearsing for the filming of the show.

Two wheeling between poles during rehearsal for filming that night.

Dinner with the Chinese stunt team after filming the show.

I asked for a water. It was hot. Another drink? A tea. I can drink tea but I usually put a lot of sugar in it. They poured something hot but it tasted like nothing I recognised as tea. There was no soft drink.

Then they brought out the food. A lot of food on a lazy Susan. There was nothing there that you could find on the menu at Junee's Nine and Ten takeaway. No-one could eat until I had taken something. I found a vegetable I figured wouldn't kill me and everyone else started. Sophia was more adventurous. As we headed back for more practice I was thinking, 'I'm going to starve in four days at this rate.'

The local drivers were getting ready for a stunt show with precision driving but, watching them, I realised their skill levels weren't high. I spoke with the interpreter and learned they did the Guinness show each year and were sponsored by the truck company and Chery. They had good cars and race suits and looked very polished but they were disorganised. They listened politely and seemed to appreciate it when I offered a few tips.

A huge drum band rehearsed in a far corner. I stood there in the enormous factory under a smoggy sky with drone cameras flying around and thought it was all surreal. It was a big production.

Crisp competition

After a few more hours practice they took us to where we were staying, in an area more like a city we were familiar with: it looked like someone lived there. There was hustle and bustle. Traffic. Twenty years ago few people in China had a car. Now China is the world's largest new car market. It's not hard to tell. It was bedlam, with people everywhere and drivers cutting in front of one another.

The hotel foyer was like a five star Hilton. It was over the top. Once in our room Sophia and I just lapped up the luxury … until I opened the curtains and looked out onto a slum. Satellite dishes held down by bricks. Broken furniture. Washing everywhere. In one direction everything was beautiful; in the other was the sobering reality of poverty.

I struggled with dinner again and sought help from the interpreter. We found a supermarket near the hotel where I tried to describe chips and soft drink. When we found the 'crisps' section I discovered they didn't have chicken flavour. They didn't have salt and vinegar. Duck. Snake. Everything but anything I knew. Just pick something, Lawrence. I did. And some soft drink. The driver paid for it. I got back to our hotel room and started eating chips. I thought it was the happiest day of my life. They actually weren't too bad. But they weren't going to last long. The next morning there was a Western breakfast. 'Hallelujah,' I thought, 'I'm not going to die.'

We loaded up the van and headed back to the venue for another half day of driving. Lunch was at a different restaurant and I had some fried rice and other things I knew to be Chinese food. And there was soft drink. I had a great meal.

After afternoon rehearsals we moved to a different hotel. It wasn't as luxurious but, apart from some things like eggs with the chickens in them, the food wasn't too strange and I didn't starve.

I had done so much rehearsing in the previous two days my arms were hurting.

My original two-wheeling record in 2005 was between two parked cars. This time they had two poles hanging down from scaffolding. Every time we touched them they swung out and had to be re-set. We got it down close to the record. The cars the Chinese drivers were using were different than mine and the gap they were driving through was larger so they had to move the poles whenever I practised.

I was getting close to the record during practice and Sophia took photos so I could see what I needed to adjust. I remembered talking to the guy from the United Kingdom who broke the record in 2009. He drove a car between two obstacles with only a forty-eight centimetre gap. I met him when he was in Australia as part of the Top Gear stunt team. He said he didn't want to attempt to break his own record because he had taken it to the absolute limit and would need to turn the car so sharply it would roll on its roof. Looking at the videos of my rehearsals I realised there was no way I could get through the poles.

We rehearsed for the start of the show, where we'd appear three cars abreast and approach the drum band, arranged with three gaps between the rows of drummers, twenty deep. They wanted us to come at the drummers backwards at sixty kilometres an hour, spin the cars around and drive between the rows of people. There must be a very relaxed attitude to occupational health and safety in China.

I was in the middle. Sitting next to me was the host of the show, who could speak English. The woman from Guinness World Records also spoke English, better than my interpreter.

We were waiting in a line and the Coach was on the radio. They were talking in Chinese but I could hear, "Hua, Chun Lin, Lawrence … go!" I stamped on the gas and we were off. Because I had the tyres pumped up hard for two-wheeling, my car wasn't sweeping the nose around quick enough. I would get out of shape and have to straighten up to race between the drummers. Then they wanted us to do a handbrake turn in line with each other as we came out the other side, right in front of the cameras. I would hop out and let the host out of the car and she would introduce the show.

While we were sitting three abreast ready to do more rehearsals, swinging between the band and trying not to kill anyone, I looked across and noticed one of the other drivers had a cable hanging from his front shocks. I realised the Chinese guys had done what the UK driver had done to break the record.

But no-one had done my car. I was competing against them and they weren't playing fair.

After the rehearsal, we were waiting to one side and I said to my interpreter, 'You need to know they have their springs cabled up.'

He said, 'What do you mean?'

'When the car goes up on two wheels, the spring will release and the wheel will stick out further. They are cabling it so when the car goes up the wheel stays in position, making the car smaller. My car isn't done like that.'

He said, 'That's not right' and went over to talk to the producer of the show. The producer then tore the Coach a new fundament. There was lots of talk. I said I would still do it the way it was but the interpreter said they would fix my car. They didn't have time to do it properly but I let them try.

Thousands of people turned up on the night of the show. There were people everywhere. Sophia was amazed at the applause I received in such an enormous venue. She said it was as if I was a god, up on a pedestal. It was the first time she had seen me in that light. She sat with the beautiful Chinese girls, who told her how amazing they thought I was. There were bright lights, the noise, the drums, the dragons — it was huge. It vibrated all through her.

The other drivers started off with some precision driving and I took the host for a two-wheel. I let her out and while she was talking to camera I drove past and handed her a rose.

The meat of the show was the attempt at the Guinness World Record. I asked my interpreter to tell the other drivers I didn't care who got the record as long as one of us got it. According to the rules, we were supposed to have three attempts each. The Chinese guys went first but no-one could squeeze through the gap. I thought I might be in with a chance but had a couple of goes with no success. After three runs each none of us had got it so the organisers threw the Guinness regulations out the window and gave me another three attempts. The Chinese guys gave me the thumbs up; they wanted me to get the record. On one pass I just clipped a pole with my rear wheel. I was centimetres away from breaking the record.

Photos were taken at the end. They had certificates printed and medals minted in case any of us succeeded. In the evening we went back to a big function hall at the hotel. Guests were seated around large tables in separate rooms. I was with the producers of the show, the owner of the truck company, the woman from Guinness World Records and my interpreter. In the next room were the stunt drivers, in another room were other precision drivers and in another room still were the drivers that took us around.

Everyone was celebrating the occasion with wine and spirits. Even though I don't drink I couldn't be impolite so had a small glass into which they poured a pricey brew from a little bottle in a fancy box. There were toasts. Lots of toasts. And after our meal and photos with people in our room I had to move on and have toasts with the other drivers, still in their race suits. As I moved from room to room I was having the smallest of sips but my throat was starting to burn. It was horrible.

More photos were taken. Everyone had a good time. The Coach asked me back to coordinate some stunts. The owner of the trucking company wanted to give me a prime mover; left hand drive of course.

It was a bizarre experience but something I'd never take back.

We thanked everyone and went to bed. The next morning we had breakfast and flew out.

When you get up in the morning you never know what the day is going to bring. You don't know what emails will arrive or what phone calls you'll get.

17

Rebirth of a Legend

My life has shifted dramatically. The goal I'm striving toward has changed since I started my career. I have stepped away from bikes, moved to the cars, and returned to the bikes — my true love. The next stage of my career was a matter of fighting with myself about how I was going to do it or if I wanted to do it.

I have experienced a rebirth that reminded me of the passion all those years ago. It was almost washed away by the negativity in recent years but now the drive is even stronger.

Things are different than they were twenty-five years ago; I'm no longer a youthful eighteen year old. I am a lot more focused, more business oriented and aware of what needs to be done, not just what I *think* needs to be done. I have surrounded myself with professional people who can help me achieve my goals.

The death of my father has changed things as well. He was my inspiration, the one who always said no matter what you want to do, keep on driving forward. I always bounced ideas off him. Even if I didn't always listen to him, he was someone to talk to.

We didn't always agree; he came from an era where you made do with what you had and kept going, whereas now making do will not be sufficient: I want everything to be one hundred per cent polished. This is my last chance to capture the imagination of the audience I have always dreamed of attracting.

Things must be methodical this time around. Everything has been carefully considered, from deciding at the beginning of 2014 what I wanted to do, to how I was going to achieve it, deciding to obtain some Harley-Davidsons, financing the bikes and then everything to support it — marketing and merchandise.

I am a firm believer that everything happens for a reason and that steps are there for us to follow. Sometimes we just take the long way around. I feel that I have gone the long way but now there is one clear path and I'm being pushed down it hard.

It's not about doing bigger stunts, not to do better than anyone else or to copy other people's stunts. It's about reimagining the whole genre; taking bits from the Evel Knievel days, from the eighties, from the nineties, from my career, all combined to create a new foundation for Lawrence Legend.

A story to tell

When Evel Knievel was jumping people were much more innocent, they didn't have social media; if you did something and it appeared in a newspaper the world knew about it — that was the news. Now you can do something and fifty thousand people will like it on Facebook but that is as far as it goes. And you are competing with tens of thousands of other people looking for attention — whatever people are interested in that second; not that week, not that day but that second.

That's why there will never be another Evel Knievel or another Dale Buggins. In their time attention was focused on one spot; today it fans out.

The more I look back at the photos and videos from those 'golden years' the more I appreciate the way Evel Knievel spoke to the audience, the way he gave interviews. He had a story to tell each time; it was more about the story than it was about the stunt. People are interested in a good story; the stunt is the kernel but there should be a lot more wrapped around it.

I don't think my age is a factor, except psychologically. People will say someone is too old to do something; Australians are good at telling people they aren't good enough, even if they are in their prime. If you are too young you are not experienced, there's someone old who can do it better; when you are older you are too old and there is someone younger who can do it better. It comes down to your body: if you are fit and healthy and if your mind is focused, age isn't a factor.

Evel Knievel was still touring with his son into his forties and Bubba Blackwell — the American stunt performer who broke Evel Knievel's jump records for cars and buses using a Harley-Davidson XR-750 — is still going at forty-eight. So I reckon I can push fifty comfortably.

Up to when he was in his seventies and he started getting sick, you could still find my Dad up on the roof or pulling down a wall. I can see myself two-wheeling and doing the fun things into my seventies. If I keep my faculties.

I can see I am just putting myself in the firing line for people compelled to doubt and criticise me. In recent years there has been less of that because I haven't been in the public eye. Now there is the possibility I could be humiliated. It was an emotional struggle to comes to terms with that and weigh it against what I want to achieve.

In the old days I was always trying to break a record, to make myself known. Now I am known; I have an extensive list of achievements. I could think that I have nothing more to achieve and I should leave it alone. But then I see the guys who say, 'I used to be awesome, go and see me on YouTube.' I'm not ready to be on one of those shows: *Where are they now?*

When I appeared on *The Footy Show* with Laurie Daley — the two Lauries from Junee — it was around the time of his retirement. He said he couldn't believe I was still doing it.

I understand that injuries prevent a lot of sportspeople from continuing with their careers but many also reach a peak, achieve

A very proud father (Reg) standing alongside me after I had jumped two buses lengthwise.

Leaping over my own home in Junee (1999).

Jumping over an airborne plane was very challenging. This was filmed for a Canadian TV show.

On 'The Footy Show' with football legend Laurie Daley (far right) also from Junee.

all their goals, and peter out because there is nothing to drive them further. If you don't have that drive and determination you will never get to the high point of your career, sport or any other activity.

I feel like Madonna, reinventing myself: from motorbikes to cars, from cars to Harleys. It's the same with any entertainer; it's why Miley Cyrus, a Disney icon, shaves her head and walks around with next to nothing on; she'll be going in a different direction when she's older.

But that's just the surface. You can't change what is. I've always been a stuntman. I have spoken to a lot of stunt performers over the years; there aren't too many who have said, 'I wanted to be a stuntman when I was a kid; now I am one.' It's usually accidental, or incidental; they saw an ad in a paper and thought it would be interesting.

Anyone can do what I do. But it takes drive and dedication to get off your backside, set everything up, make banners, make fliers, tell people to come to your jumps, do the stunt, get paid and go home. Anyone can do the stunt. It's what's required before and after the jump that's the hard work. There are plenty of people who can do my job better than I can. The difference is my determination to make it happen. That's how it has always been.

That's who I am and who I will be.

18

Always Believe in Your Dreams

People either love them or hate them. For some people they are like a status symbol.

I have wanted a Harley-Davidson ever since I was a kid when Mum bought raffle tickets so I might win one. As I grew older I had other priorities. A Harley-Davidson would come later. So March 2014 was the first time I even sat on a Harley, let alone rode one.

The Harley XR-750 was the bike I wanted. It was a very successful racing bike and of course the favourite motorcycle of Evel Knievel. I knew they were too expensive but always in the back of my mind was, 'Harley, Harley, Harley. How can I do this?' For a while I visited bike shops just to admire them without looking at prices. I was the typical wannabe Harley rider: no bike just T-shirts and hats. Even when I could afford one I put my money back into the stunts. Harleys were a luxury. My early jumping bike, the Honda CB360 with a twin cylinder and a nice big note to it, was a poor man's Harley.

Early in my relationship with Sophia, when we took a trip to Melbourne, we went into a Harley shop. Sophia was struck by the smell of the tyres, the shiny chrome, all the bikes lined up … and the look of excitement on my face. I was drawn straight over to a bright orange XR-750 on display. It wasn't hard for Sophia to feel my enthusiasm as I talked to her about the bike and explained that was what Evel Knievel used to jump. It was one of the first times she saw how passionate I was about my stunt work.

She said she had loved Harleys ever since she was taken on a Harley ride during a holiday in Cairns. When I told her about my goal to own one she said, 'You know you are going to own a Harley one day. I can see it happening for you.' I thought she might be buying me one. She bought me a Harley-Davidson shirt for my birthday.

When I still wanted to get a road bike she said, 'No, you don't want that. You just wait until you get your Harley.' But I needed something to ride — part of that mid-life crisis desire to go riding on the roads. I once said I'd never ride a bike on the road because it was too dangerous. Another idiot would wipe me out. Don't worry about getting killed doing a bike stunt jumping over something; the end would come when some clown didn't stop at a traffic light.

So I got a Honda CBR600 and took Sophia for a ride. She loved it at the time but the CBR600 is a sports racing bike. It went fast enough and was good for me to be on by myself but was not ideal with a passenger.

On subsequent trips to Melbourne we visited the Harley shop, still dreaming of owning one — not for jumps but to ride around. The price was prohibitive. They were expensive enough to begin with but, after adding some nice grips or shiny bits or changing the exhaust system or putting saddle bags on it, you'd spend another five thousand dollars before you left the shop. The dealer would make more money selling accessories than by selling motorbikes. Sophia bought a jacket and some other merchandise but I went online and found a jacket that could be shipped from the United States for half the price. I had the jacket but still no Harley. And I couldn't wear the jacket riding my Honda.

It was sheer coincidence that I was selling a motocross bike and happened to mention that I was after a Harley. The guy buying my old bike asked if I was interested in a Harley-Davidson Sportster.

'Sure!'

His price was me giving him my bike plus some cash — which defeated the purpose because I was looking for cash, not trying to get rid of it. But he said he collected motorbikes and was interested in older models. I said I had a shed full of bits of pieces from the seventies and eighties. So we struck a deal that saw him with a trailer load of bike parts.

When we made the swap Sophia said, 'You're giving a trailer load of crap for that nice shiny bike on the back of his ute?'

'Yes.'

'Well make the swap quickly before he changes his mind.'

I had a Harley-Davidson.

We loved the freedom of cruising on a Harley. With a Harley-Davidson you could take your time on the back roads. I didn't like traffic around me. I could be by myself. I was already looking at getting a bigger and better one that was even more comfortable for cruising.

The dream, though, was not just to ride a Harley-Davidson; it was to jump one. And not just any Harley; it had to be the XR-750.

The problem remained the price of the bikes. They were not cheap. Due to relatively low production numbers and recent interest in them as investments they could cost anything from fifteen to forty thousand dollars. No bike is worth that amount of money, let alone a bike to be used for jumping.

Another obstacle was that the XR-750 is a race bike that can't be purchased in Australia as a complete bike. You can buy only the engine from Harley-Davidson, in over two hundred pieces you must assemble yourself. Then you buy the frame and wheels and build the rest of the bike.

I had to bide my time. And work on my dream.

When I first performed at Royal Easter Shows with the Toyota team I imagined they would be the perfect place to jump Harleys. I knew you had to be on and off very quickly so visualised rolling out matting off the back of a ute to give the bike traction. The jumps could be set up quickly. I could come out, do some wheelies, do the jump and it all could be pulled down again with little fuss.

While I was mapping this out in my head I became friends with the woman who ran the entertainment for the Sydney Show. She was looking for new acts and knew I performed stunts so I asked her what she thought about Harley-Davidson jumps like in the days of Evel Knievel. She said it sounded interesting and asked me to send her information about it. I thought that was a bit premature but talked to one of my bosses. He had a fair bit of money and I thought he might be interested in branching out. He must have done the maths about what a couple of bikes would cost — and he probably didn't want to lose me from the team and then have me as a competitor. That conversation didn't progress. Without the financial backing I couldn't pursue it further.

I emailed Bubba Blackwell and asked if I could call him. It had been seven years since I had last spoken to him. At the time he told me how hard it was to get an XR-750. I told him what I wanted to do but said I didn't want to tread on his toes. He said if anyone was to do it he wanted it to be me. I should be doing it in Australia. In that case, I said, could he give me some help finding a bike? He put out some feelers and came across Jess Roeder, 1998 American Motorcyclist Association Champion and son of famous Harley-Davidson factory racer George Roeder.

As soon as I started talking to Jess I knew he was someone I could trust. His family had been in the motorcycle business for many years. We got to talking about the bike I was after and he said he had two. Within that half-hour conversation I had agreed to take both of them ... not knowing how I was going to find the money. As fortune would have it, he said they were all in parts and it would take a few months to put them back together. I thought that would give me time to raise the money but he said he wanted half up front. I got off the phone in a bit of a sweat wondering what I had done. Sophia said, 'You'll be right. The money will be there if you need it.'

So I started to make phone calls. I had an old American classic car. I texted a guy who replied within two minutes saying one of his employees had just been asking where he could find such a car. After that I sold everything I had surplus to my needs: trucks, cars, motorbikes. Anything that wasn't bolted down. The money started falling into my lap.

All the things that had accumulated over twenty-five years were literally and figuratively being cleared from my path. But there were still obstacles to negotiate.

It took six months for the bikes to be rebuilt. Then I had to organise shipping. The first shipping company proved the truth of the adage 'You get what you pay for'. I found them through a full-page ad in a magazine. They said they were experienced but clearly weren't experienced enough. It was a nightmare. They said they couldn't ship the bikes because they didn't have frame numbers and they wanted to cart a bike from Ohio to Los Angeles on the back of an open car carrier. Three months later, after a long exchange of emails, I turned to another company that advertised in the same magazine. They guaranteed they could get the bikes into Australia without frame numbers because they were solely race bikes, not to be registered for riding on roads.

Meanwhile, one bike was still sitting in Ohio. It only took a week to get it to Los Angeles via San Diego but we missed the November departure date by one day. That was extremely frustrating, especially considering it cost me more to move the bikes from one side of America to the other than it did to ship them to Australia.

That delay, with strikes, staff shortages and not enough trucks to move containers in and out of the port, meant I had to wait another month. Then, after arriving in Australia, it took four weeks for the bikes to clear Customs. It would be nearly twelve months since speaking with Jess Roeder that I could sit astride my XR-750s.

A Harley-Davidson XR-750, the same type of bike Evel Knievel used. This is the XR in the Harley shop in Melbourne that Sophia and I saw and which effected a rebirth of my love for jumping bikes.

The Honda CRR600, the first real road bike I rode for stress release.

It took over 30 years but I finally got my first Harley-Davidson.

Following my heroes

Finally I had the Harley-Davidsons and the time was right for me to work with them. I had followed the history of the Harley legends — all the old videos of my heroes that I'd watched over and over again — and could now pay tribute to them.

One aspect of that tribute I hoped had already been achieved: every daredevil has to have a horrible crash.

The XR-750s might be nice looking bikes and the loud, deep rumble — as opposed to the high pitch of a motocross bike — might get the crowds excited but they are hard to jump because they were made for dirt track racing and not for flying. On film footage of Evel Knievel or Bubba Blackwell you can see them landing sideways because there is so much torque they come down on an angle.

Evel Knievel had many crashes but his most famous came in December 1967 when he failed in his attempt to jump the fountains at Caesars Palace, a luxury hotel and casino in Las Vegas. It was his longest attempted motorcycle jump at one hundred and forty-one feet (forty-three metres). After the crash Knievel was more famous than ever.

In February 1971, he set a new world record by jumping nineteen cars with his Harley-Davidson XR-750 at the Ontario Motor Speedway, California. He held the record for twenty-seven years until Bubba Blackwell jumped twenty cars in 1998 with an XR-750.

Bubba Blackwell, who turned to stunt riding after a successful career in road racing, attempted twenty-two cars in 2001. The ground on the horse racing track was soft and Bubba, not using a speedometer, lost traction, hit the edge of the safety deck and summersaulted over the landing ramp and onto his head. Like my Bolton Park jump and Evel Knievel's Caesars Palace jump, it could have been the accident that made him famous. He was on the news and television talk shows and it opened the door to other television shows.

John Smeaton, who runs the *Cycle Jumpers* website from Long Beach, California, says the personality needed to be a jumper is *crazy*. 'It's like a drug,' he says. 'You get addicted to the adrenalin. It's in their blood.'

Fortunately, John thinks my latest career move wasn't totally crazy.

John is a graphic designer whose hobby has been managing the *Cycle Jumpers* website. He doesn't ride himself. His only stunts have been wheelies on a bicycle. When he started the site he wanted to pick a topic that wasn't prominent on the web. He'd always been a fan of cycle jumping and, as a child, collected newspaper clippings about Evel Knievel. There was plenty of information about Evel Knievel on the web but not so much about other jumpers. In addition to Evel Knievel and English jumpers Robin Winter-Smith and Eddie Kidd, one of the first stunt riders he added to the site was me, after he had read an article in the *National Enquirer* about my 1991 accident at Bolton Park.

John says the seventies was a key decade for motorcycle jumping. There were many jumping he didn't know about until he started building his website. He knew of Bob Gill, Bob Duffey and Debbie Lawler, one of the few female jumpers, but then a lot of other people came and the list of jumpers kept growing. As is the case in Australia, some were only known in regional areas.

Jumping was popular in Australia in the mid to late seventies and early eighties with Dale Buggins and Johnny Fogwell. Robbie Madison, who has crossed over from freestyle motocross to daredevil stunts, is very well-known today — and has major sponsors. Tyrone Gilks seemed a great prospect before he died, in March 2013, aged nineteen, practising to break Maddison's 250cc distance record. Matt Coulter (known as the Kangaroo Kid) has a successful career jumping quad bikes.

John thinks the jumpers with a strong drive, and focused on what they want to do, tend to be more successful. They are good at coming up with interesting stunts and they understand the marketing end of things. Evel Knievel was a master of marketing and promoting himself. You have to be a showman and a promoter.

John points to the jumpers' uniforms he displays on his site. Each person, he says, is like their own little superhero. You can't tell who today's freestyle motorcyclists are, he says. They look the same, with sponsors' logos all over them. The traditional jumpers have unique suits and you can tell who they are.

My uniform is black with a blue field with stars and a fringe on my sleeves. Bubba has flames, with red, white and blue. You need the whole package. The jump lasts only three seconds; the rest is all about the build-up to the jump, it's after the jump, it's souvenirs and meeting with the fans.

My clean-cut image could also help. Many jumpers are tattooed up and mouth profanities without a second thought. They have trouble going far because families won't go to see them and children won't look up to them. Like Bubba Blackwell, my focus is on family entertainment and keeping a good, positive image.

Cycle jumping has a bigger market in the United States than it does in Australia. It is very popular in the mid-west and the south and generally is more successful drawing crowds in small towns. There aren't many traditional motorcycle jumpers who do ramp-to-ramp like Evel Knievel.

One rider, Doug Danger, held the world record for the longest ramp-to-ramp jump. In 2014 he jumped with an XR-750 using modern ramps, higher and curved, which meant he didn't need to be as fast because he attained a higher altitude.

Bubba Blackwell uses low kick-off ramps like those used by Evel Knievel. His ramps require the bike to go fast and low over the cars, which makes it dangerous.

There is a debate in the daredevil community about who is more authentic (Evel Knievel-like): the riders with modern suspension or those with little shocks like Knievel and hardly any clearance on the seat; the riders using the low ramps or the riders using the curved ramps.

Bubba Blackwell might be the only one who still does it full-time for a living. Others do it for fun or to supplement another income. It also comes in phases; freestyle motorcycles were popular for a while, with the Crusty Demons films and freestyle motocross. After a while even their backflips were done so often they became boring. There are plenty of places now — YouTube and extreme bike movies— where people can see riders falling off bikes. An old-school stunt show is something different. And I shouldn't be as likely to kill myself. That's important because I don't bounce like I used to.

In the United States there has been a resurgence of interest in traditional motorcycle jumping, especially since plans were made to jump the Snake River Canyon, forty years after Evel Knievel's failed attempt in September 1974. The distances might not be as far but there is still excitement when you realise the cyclist isn't landing on a mountain of dirt but on small wooden ramps. Plus there is the nostalgia factor.

Before I got the XR-750s the bikes we used for crashing into cars were just old Japanese bikes (no-one seems to like Japanese bikes). I managed to do seventeen head-on crashes with one bike before the frame was so bent I couldn't use it anymore and had to retire it.

When the front forks bend you take them out and put them in a big press, straighten the fork, buy another wheel from the wreckers and away you go. Of course they don't steer real well after the tenth crash and they track a bit funny. I try to recycle as much as I can.

I need to treat my Harleys better than that; they cost a bit more.

I first got people's attention jumping a big, heavy road bike. My career will continue grabbing people's attention jumping Harleys. And there are plenty of Harley riders — businessmen, lawyers, bikies — who will come to watch because they are Harley-Davidsons. Because they just hate Japanese bikes.

19
YOU WON'T BELIEVE WHAT I DO NEXT

Being a daredevil is in my DNA. I'm not saying it's a strong personal preference. DNA could well be motivating my risk-taking behaviour.

Scientific studies suggest my urge to launch myself off ramps is not just attention seeking — my genes could have made me 'sensation seeking'. According to the research, some people might have an innate, inherited need to turn to risky activities like hurtling over rows of buses even if their parents are quiet, respectable types, like Mum and Dad. For one thing, that would explain my childhood craving for large amounts of physical stimulation.

Whether they're a BASE jumper, skydiver, high-wire walker, skier, snowboarder, human cannonball, motorbike jumper or some other kind of extreme athlete, one thing all daredevils have in common is their willingness to put their lives on the line. For some, it might not actually be that dangerous — but the more reckless it looks the better.

People like to watch daredevils in action for a vicarious thrill (it's something they'd never be game to attempt) or in hope of witnessing a spectacular crash. For many daredevils, though, it's not about the size of the audience or the publicity or the records. They can do what they do in front of small audiences or even for their own amusement. They're there for a heady brew of adrenalin, experimentation and personal examination.

I like speed; it intrigues me. However, there's a special thrill to jumping. Attempting the feat scares me but I'm still attracted by the thought of doing it. Even though before a jump the adrenalin is flowing and I'm nervous, there's always the rush when I've completed it and the thought that maybe no-one else has done what I've just done.

Perhaps that's a gift, seeing the daredevils who have paved the way, seeing if there were any mistakes, if there is a way to improve on a stunt. It's great to do something that hasn't been done before. It's also good to make an old stunt even better. Someone will probably look at my stunts and think they can be done better. The old ways still seem to work pretty well but you can always look for an opportunity to progress an idea.

I have videos of the stunt guys from the seventies, high end stunt coordinators for movies, and what they were doing was very similar to what I was doing with ramps in the dirt in my backyard. Even today some stunts use ramps wedged into the ground so when the bike hits them it kicks up and loses momentum and what they call preload. The ramps used for backflips, though, are curved so the bike comes up smoothly and jumps high.

People criticise me, saying I have done a lot of stunts that haven't worked. But I say it's not because of my skill levels; it's because I didn't have the time and resources to make them work. And, in any case, my failures usually made the jumps more spectacular.

Improvements in technology and corporate funding have made some jumps easier. The spiral jump I attempted has now been achieved a couple of times. One driver used a different technique to make the vehicle spin. They had an off-road truck with long suspension and a normal ramp. But at the top of the ramp was a peak that the front wheel hit and spun the car. The suspension absorbed the impact and the car drove off.

Another guy, who successfully made the spiral jump with a Chevrolet Sonic, was a skateboarder with huge financial backing. He used stuntmen to practise the stunt until they had it down to a fine art.

Then they strapped him in and put him in front of the cameras. He took the glory but someone had been there and done it all to make his job easy. Those stunt guys did a dozen odd jumps before the star got even close to sitting in the car.

If you have unlimited money or time there's nothing you can't do.

But me, I had one car and wrote it off.

A key part of coming back is that people who were there in 1991 and watched me again in 2000 will have kids themselves who can watch me just like their dad or mum did. Perhaps seeing someone from a small town with the kind of success I have found will give young guys with pushbikes and motorbikes an incentive to have a go themselves.

It's a lot harder being a public figure, entertainer or celebrity now than it was back then, however. Unfortunately, our country is fertile ground for naysayers and knockers. Australians are good at holding their stars in high regard but as soon as their idols are not doing well they derive some dark satisfaction from trampling all over them. In America and China people treat you like rock stars and think you are wonderful but here you're just an ego-driven tosser. It can be very disheartening.

It's magic

When I finished with the Toyota HiLux team I tried to get out and about with my family and do some active things like hiking to waterfalls, not just sitting and watching television. My son James and I have a good relationship because I'm just a big kid at heart. He loves the superheroes and action heroes that I always loved. Any sort of action movie. The only thing I can't do with him is play video games because I get nauseous from the quick movement and things going on in the background. I haven't moved on since Space Invaders.

I tried racing games and used to enjoy the simpler arcade rally games but I can't sit down at a computer with car simulation games. Apart from giving me migraines they annoy me. I don't have the touch and feel feedback I need. I bought a game called *Stuntman*, where you can create stunts and movie scenes. I got fed up with that within hours: it's easier to do the stunt than it is to play it on the damn console. I liked the concept, though. It had a free-range option where you could build stunts in an arena — that was fun because I could create stunts I couldn't create in real life.

There are quite a few stunt and daredevil games, even an Evel Knievel game, but there isn't one that does the stunts the way I think they should be done. It seems that what I see and what other people see are totally different. My imagination and hands-on approach would make it more realistic, rather than how a game designer *thinks* a daredevil should be.

Stunt performances, like the games, are a bit of escapism. They are a lot like magic shows. People want to know how it's done. Sometimes there's a high percentage of illusion and a small part is talent. To be successful you have to be as much an entertainer as you are a performer. Some might not have any skills but, gee, they are interesting to watch!

I heard of a guy attempting to replicate an Evel Knievel stunt and filming himself during practice. That's a mistake; it detracts from the stunt. People need to think you haven't practised beforehand, that you have just turned up on the day and are about to attempt something crazy. If they know you are going to make it, that ruins the daredevil act. Even if you have spent two months rehearsing, people want to think you are reckless. People want it to be absolutely amazing or a huge train wreck.

I understand the desire to be filmed, however. I always had a passion for photography — the idea of being able to capture something, a certain moment. I like to picture something before it happens, how

Checking over the XR750s after their arrival from the USA.

One boy very happy to have his Harley-Davidson XR-750s here in Australia.

Publicity shot for upcoming stunts (2014)

A new chapter: chasing my childhood dream again.

it needs to be. The subject matter I want to shoot is the jumps I do but, since I can't be in front of the camera and behind the camera at the same time, I have tried to tell my friends how they should be shooting the stunts. They thought I was just being difficult but they usually came to understand why some angles were better than others. I'd hate to be a movie director, trying to communicate my vision to a film crew.

I quickly learned the importance of photography, especially before video and YouTube. The still photograph was the thing people saw and remembered you by. If you didn't have a great picture you missed out. Back then, with 35 mm film, you didn't know if you got the right shot or not. Unless you had an expensive camera with a motor drive you were in the hands of the gods. You could make an awesome jump only to find you were half out of the frame.

When I jumped in my prime, before the GoPros, I had to carry a bumbag with a recorder and fit a POV camera to my helmet. When I jumped the aeroplane I had the camera in a backpack. I'm sure it wouldn't have helped if I crashed.

My jump at Junee Show in 1989 was filmed by a mate's father using one of the first 'affordable' cameras, released in 1988 for the Australian bicentenary and priced at nearly two thousand dollars. He was the only person we knew who could afford a camera, so he, along with the TV stations, filmed my first public jump. That's the only footage I have. Nowadays, with mobile phones and GoPros, everyone's an action hero — with a little bit of editing and hundreds of hours of being stupid.

This time around we are making sure we capture the best images and our filming of course includes GoPros.

The six stunts to relaunch my career in 2015 also celebrated my quarter century as a daredevil stunt rider — creating, performing and holding over twenty Australian, world and Guinness records.

Those jumps — over a Blue Thunder helicopter gunship, a ten-seater seaplane, two double-decker buses lengthways, a large house, a locomotive train engine and the fountains of 'Monte Cristo' — were just the beginning. There are many other stunts to do; stunts to set up, control and film. I will get the records, with perfect shots, from every angle, of the perfect jumps.

I have a book that I sketch in and draw up plans for the stunts I'd love to do — stunts I think can be improved or something completely different. With the resources to bring them to life and jumping regularly, not waiting for ten or twelve months, I can make Australian or world-first jumps, attempt some old stunts with the Harleys and break some old records.

The scaffolding companies refused to build the huge landing ramp I once used for the record jumps — or else they wanted ten or twenty thousand dollars every time they put it up. I thought that was ridiculous; I'd build it on my own. But it takes a good four hours to put up that ramp with four people working on it, which is why it is so much easier doing stunts on our property: we can leave the ramps up.

My stunts might involve some danger but setting them up is the main difficulty. The stunts are something I need to control to make sure the timing is right, so they are done right. I can't be under the pressure of having a four-hour set up and a fifteen-minute window to get a stunt done. It just wouldn't work.

I'm putting the Ring of Fire back in the show. It isn't very difficult or clever but it used to feature in the old shows and it appears dangerous. It looks cool. It sounds exciting.

I saw a sign recently quoting French novelist Anatole France: 'To accomplish great things we must not only act but also dream; not only plan but also believe.' You can't achieve anything great by just being good at something. You have to have the passion to see it through.

I want to do the stunts I envisage before my time is up. I don't want to look back and think, 'If I just pushed myself a bit harder I could have done that stunt. It would have been easy. It would have looked great.'

People say I could make a lot of money out of stunt work. But what they call a lot of money isn't what I call success. Success is doing what I plan. I've just had to take the long route sometimes. My wealth will be being able to buy 'Monte Cristo', build the Stuntman and Daredevil Hall of Fame, and live the rest of my life with a smile on my face.

'This is what I did.'

'This is what I am still doing.'

'Here are the great things other stunt performers have done.'

'This is where I grew up.'

'This is my father's legacy.'

All these things have a story to be told. As I'm getting older I'm beginning to feel that's what I am: a story teller; a teller of many different stories about 'Monte Cristo', stunt driving and being a daredevil.

20
THE FUTURE

I often think about the future of the stunt industry and the cycle of things. Ten years ago there was no freestyle motocross, no backflipping, no young people doing amazing leaps.

I get the feeling those manifestations of the sport have gone through their course and people, as always, are looking for something new. That something 'new' could be the daredevil days from the seventies. Trends come and go. It happens to clothing and music. I think it could again be the time of the daredevil.

Society now is so hard to please. Even America, where people are used to being entertained so easily, is a hard market. There are video games that seem more realistic than live action. There are movies with CGI and stunts that could never be achieved in real life. Young people get killed because the impossible seems possible. Life is just a game and they think there are no consequences for their actions.

The stunt industry has changed significantly but car jumping will always be car jumping and bike jumping will always be bike jumping. The difference is that there are fewer specialists. Stunt performers don't just do cars or don't just do motorbikes. The new generation of stunt performers in movies are young and fit and most of the breathtaking stunts are done by CGI or with wires and cable. The most spectacular crashes happen in a controlled environment.

Regulations are intruding into my kind of real-life stunt action. As Hal Needham said, there's no such thing as a great stunt if there's no danger involved. How can you ride through an explosion if you aren't allowed to be near the fireworks? It's not like the movies, where you can have the fireworks and digitally add the stunt performer later.

That's the magic of the live show. A mother has to explain to her child that it's not computer generated. What they can see is *actually* happening.

There are some guys who have been in the business as long as I have who still do the big car stunts but it's so technically advanced now that it's almost impossible not to do the job properly. There's everything from air cannons that punch a piston downward, causing the car to flip, to the switches that lock the brakes, and stunt teams that rehearse and practise stunts until they are perfect for the camera.

I love the daredevil stunts more. You can't fake it. You can't pretend that you're someone you're not. It's as real as it gets. When you are there to watch it live, your heart starts to race, you start to worry for the daredevil, you're not sure what the outcome will be. When you stand there and see the distance between two ramps and know that someone has to actually do that, you get excited — that's where you've invested your time and emotion.

Lawrence Legend's stunts are now performed and recorded on the 'Monte Cristo' property at Junee, where I can manage my schedule and promote the Lawrence Legend merchandise and the Stuntman Daredevil Hall of Fame.

If you're a stunt performer there's always someone trying to fleece you or make you do things you don't want to do. Promoters are only interested in the bottom dollar. They don't care what's happening in the arena, only whether they make money or don't lose money.

This time around I want to avoid that stress as much as possible. That's the good thing about doing it at home. If I don't want to do it one day, I'll get up the next day and do it. It's a lot easier. With controlled events and social media I won't be dependent on touring where other people make money from me.

The legacy and the story are important. The Hall of Fame is the result of twenty-five years of collecting memorabilia and articles of historic significance. It will include items such as movie stunt props, a 1954 Globe of Death, a human cannon and a double-decker bus. As well as preserving the amazing history of daredevil life, it will showcase stunt people from all corners of the world.

'Monte Cristo' has to be about more than antique furniture and a historic house. Every town has those. But every town doesn't have a haunted house with such a reputation.

Add to that the Stuntman Hall of Fame and it will be interesting for everyone. Even people not attracted by ghosts will be a little bit curious about it. And people not initially drawn to the stunts might be a bit curious about that too. There will always be stories to tell, something that will spark their imagination.

In the long run

There are times when people get depressed, when they can't face life; there are some horrible things going on out there. Human beings really need some way to escape. If it's going to the movies, fine. If you've come to see Lawrence Legend jump over a row of buses, that's fine. Whatever it is, it's just something to help you — for a few thrilling moments — forget the worries of the world.

Although she hasn't always liked it, Mum says she is proud of what I have done with my life. I don't see myself as anything great. I'm just Lawrence. But I've never given up, despite all the obstacles people have put in my way. I've sought to do what is right for me, to live my dream.

I'm not trying to prove how wonderful I am; I just want to entertain people, to do things that capture people's attention. That's what the definition of stunt is: an act or a feat done to attract attention.

Media attention for stunts at 'Monte Cristo' has fluctuated over the years, from the times when I would call and reporters would come out to times it depended on their roster or they wanted us to send them

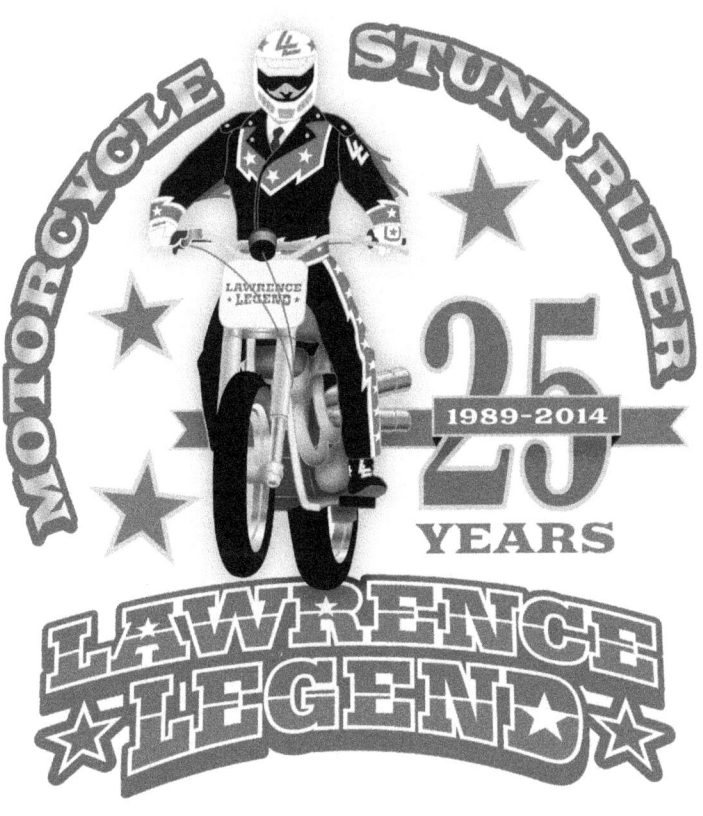

Twenty-five years and still going strong. And some people said I wouldn't make it past my 21st birthday!

You can't get much happier than this, smiling from ear to ear. Lawrence Legend and one of his new Harley-Davidson XR-750s.

Things are going to start jumping around here. My only wish was that my Dad could have been here to see it.

our own photographs. With public relations and news agencies it was almost easier to get our stories in international media than in the local newspaper. With age and time come respect and perhaps now I will be taken more seriously. As I relaunch my career those people who thought I was dead and gone may remember me and come to see what's happening.

I have ten years left to do things on my bucket list; I mightn't achieve them all but at least I'm not going to be fifty-five and wishing I tried a bit harder.

You should never regret anything but it would be horrible to sit back and think you didn't do the things you wanted. I might have to work until the day I die but until then I am going to enjoy myself.

I love the quote from Hunter S. Thompson: 'Life should not be a journey to the grave with the intention of arriving safely in a pretty and well preserved body, but rather to skid in broadside in a cloud of smoke, thoroughly used up, totally worn out and loudly proclaiming "Wow! What a Ride!"'

That's how life should be lived. Riding high.

My friend Charlie Ford once said something that could well serve as an epitaph: 'Lawrence Ryan: No fear or no brains. An entertainer. He just wanted to put on a show.'

I still do! And, as my time's not up just yet, the show will go on.

In a 1980 documentary Evel Knievel said, 'Being an American daredevil is the shortest profession you could choose; you'll be a hero one day and forgotten the next.'

Today, with YouTube, someone's fifteen minutes of fame could last less than a minute. But, unlike something on YouTube that gets a million hits and is instantly forgotten, people can come and see my stunts, get a sense of what is really happening and perhaps the memory will last longer. As Evel Knievel said, 'If you think what I did today was amazing, wait until you see what I do tomorrow.'

Dad believed in me from day dot and I'm disappointed he wasn't here to see the Harleys arrive and to see the new stunts. He knew how much I was longing to jump Harleys.

I'm pretty sure he's still watching.

www.ingramcontent.com/pod-product-compliance
Ingram Content Group UK Ltd.
Pitfield, Milton Keynes, MK11 3LW, UK
UKHW021300180426
11947UKWH00015B/941